CW00419867

TRAVELLING TOGETHER

A handbook on Local Ecumenical Partnerships

Elizabeth Welch and Flora Winfield

with information on Wales by
Gethin Abraham-Williams

CTE (Publications)
Inter-Church House
35-41 Lower Marsh
London SE1 7RL

"As we travel the way of Pilgrims we must continue to study together the important issues that divide us (eg. the nature of the church, authority, ministry) and celebrate the gift of that unity which we have already received."

(from *The Swanwick Declaration*, 1987)

ISBN 1 874295 09 3

© Welch and Winfield
Cover design by Ray Liberty
Printed by Gem Publishing Company
Wallingford, Oxon.
Published by CTE (Publications)
Inter-Church House
35-41 Lower Marsh
London SE1 7RL

CONTENTS

FOREWORD

The frequent use of the word 'ecumenism' gives the impression that we are dealing with something static and incapable of change. The truth is that we are being caught up more and more into the ecumenical **movement.** We are pilgrims on a journey to a distant goal, passing thorough landscape which changes as we travel together. It is not only the landscape which is changing, but ourselves, although we do not always see the changes until some time after they have taken place.

So it is with Local Ecumenical Partnerships (LEPs). For those who have been pioneers from the earliest days of 'areas of ecumenical experiment', and those who have shared the life of 'local ecumenical projects' over a number of years, the publication of a new book designed to help folk develop LEPs, much of what is here will seem almost too familiar to read! But the need for this book lies not in helping old hands see the way they have come, but to point out the way to the future for those newly setting their foot on the road.

LEPs have changed over the years. They were tentative at the beginning and a bit precious, but as the years have passed and their confidence has grown with their numbers, so they have come to make a number of significant changes to the life of the churches which sponsored them. Far from being the tender plants of yesterday, they continue to demonstrate that they are the foretaste of what is to come, the first fruits of that unity for which we all seek.

Those who have long experience of LEPs, no less than those who come new to them, will welcome this new publication, latest in a long line of handbooks designed to make the path of the ecumenical movement smoother. We are deeply indebted to Elizabeth Welch and Flora Winfield for this very useful and handy guide.

HUGH CROSS
Forum Moderator
Churches Together in England

June 1995

AUTHORS' PREFACE

The Rev. Elizabeth Welch

My interest in ecumenism goes back to my childhood days in South Africa. My father was a minister and so I went to church from an early age and yet, also from an early age, I experienced the deep divisions of apartheid. I began to discover for myself that the reconciliation at the heart of the Christian Gospel stood as a clear challenge to the doctrines which underlay apartheid. From those early days, I have been passionately committed to models of living that brought people together rather than separated people one from another.

Since I was ordained a minister in the United Reformed Church in April 1976, I have worked in Local Ecumenical Partnerships. For the first seven years of my ministry I served in St Barnabas' United Church and Christian Centre in Langney, Eastbourne. This was a Baptist/Methodist/URC Local Ecumenical Partnership on a new housing estate. Since 1983 I have worked in the centre of Milton Keynes at the Church of Christ the Cornerstone, which involves five denominations: Anglican/Baptist/ Methodist/Roman Catholic/United Reformed Church. Since 1991 I have served on the Central Committee of the World Council of Churches. The WCC brings together more than 300 churches from over 130 countries.

The Rev. Flora Winfield

I became involved in local ecumenism as an ordinand, working on placements in an Anglican/Baptist/Methodist/URC Local Ecumenical Partnership in Gloucester and a URC church in Wheatley, Oxfordshire. After ordination as a deacon in the Anglican church, I went as a curate to serve in the Stantonbury Ecumenical Parish in Milton Keynes, an ecumenical partnership which includes Anglicans, Baptists, Methodists, the URC, the Roman Catholic Church and the Salvation Army, and where I also worked alongside people from Black-majority churches. The breadth of ecumenical life in Milton Keynes is remarkable, but my experience of being a minister there was not of a group of Christians who were so devoted to ecumenism that there was no space for mission. Rather, I worked with people who were concerned with the task of building the kingdom and sharing the gospel in that community, and for whom the imperative for ecumenical living was the gospel imperative of that task.

I was then appointed as the first County Ecumenical Officer to Gloucestershire, where I worked on behalf of eight denominations to encourage ecumenical development and provide support and encouragement for twenty existing Local Ecumenical Partnerships and eighteen local Churches Together groups. In 1994, I was ordained to the priesthood in the Anglican church, and now serve as Chaplain to Mansfield College, Oxford, a college of URC foundation. I also serve on the General Synod's Council for Christian Unity, and on the Enabling Group of Churches Together in England.

Together

The experience we have had of working ecumenically, while not without its deep difficulties at times has been immensely enriching. It has both strengthened our understanding and valuing of our own traditions and enabled us to see our traditions as part of a wider spectrum, with which it has been vital to go on developing and deepening relationships.

When discussing our different experiences in local ecumenism, we both felt that it would be good to try and put some of these experiences in writing in order to clarify for ourselves and others working in local ecumenism the issues and ideas that form the backdrop to our local experience. We wrote this book not as people who have the answers, but as people who have been trying to draw together some of the threads of ecumenism in the hope that our experience may in some small way help the experience of others who are at different stages on the same road.

1. INTRODUCTION

Why Write this Handbook?

Local Ecumenical Partnerships have mushroomed in England and Wales in recent years – something viewed as an exciting phenomenon in the international, ecumenical scene. Only in New Zealand and Canada is there anything approaching such a scale of development in local ecumenism, although LEPs are beginning to emerge in a number of other countries. Speakers have been invited from England and Wales to tell about their experience and several articles have been written and shared internationally.

However, it does not always seem that this international enthusiasm for local ecumenism is matched within England and Wales. Sometimes LEPs are seen as problem areas that take up too much time and energy both of those participating in them and of the denominations involved. Sometimes an LEP feels isolated because it is the only one in a particular area. Sometimes it seems that there are so many things to be thought about in entering into an ecumenical partnership that it would be easier to remain within the old, familiar and trusted denomination. Sometimes those in denominational hierarchies are nervous about what can seem to be a 'letting go' by the denominations into a new animal full of the uncertainties that new being holds.

In fact there is a rich wealth of experience held within LEPs, but it is not always simple for this experience to be shared, often for geographical reasons. When difficulties arise in one area it may not be easy to discover the solutions reached by people in LEPs in other parts of the country. This handbook is an endeavour to bring together some of the insights from people who have been working for many years in local ecumenism. It is offered not in the sense of giving a blueprint, but to suggest some ways in which particular issues can be tackled in any one area. It is written both to give encouragement to people grappling with the issues involved in working with local ecumenism and to give some practical suggestions of the way in which things might be developed.

Who is this Handbook for?

The authors had a variety of people in mind when writing this handbook;

- those already working in local ecumenical partnerships who are wondering where LEPs are going;
- those considering entering into a local ecumenical partnership, but who are unsure of the issues involved and how to go about it;
- those working in denominational structures who are keen to promote local ecumenism but are not sure where to start (or even those who do not believe it can be done!);
- Ecumenical Officers who are directly involved in supporting LEPs;
- sponsoring bodies who have to handle issues concerned with LEPs;
- ordinary 'people in the pews' who are interested in knowing what ecumenism is about.

(Note: see bibliography for other useful guides).

A Vision for the Future of LEPs

A Consultation of LEPs in March 1994, organised by Churches Together in England, came up with a statement which outlines a vision for the future:

"Our vision for the future of Local Ecumenical Partnerships is that they should be a local sign, symbol and foretaste of the full visible unity of the church. We want them to be places which witness to the depths of our shared Christian heritage expressed in a rich diversity of ethnic, cultural and theological traditions, and thus able to be the church for the whole community in which each one is set.

They should find their basis and motivation in a desire to glorify God together, to serve their local community, to be instruments of reconciliation, and to carry out their mission in all its aspects. Each partnership should be responsive to the context in which its theology must be worked out, tested and lived. We trust that others, who are not at the moment involved in many such partnerships, will be drawn in (e.g. the Black majority, Pentecostal, and House or New Churches).

LEPs and their parent denominations or churches have to work harder at their mutual relationships and responsibilities. LEPs need the denominations and sponsoring bodies to listen to the dilemmas and opportunities facing them and to respond with pastoral sensitivity and support. In turn LEPs are called to challenge the denominations in their separateness and also to be challenged by them to value their respective traditions.

They are to be examples of good practice and stewardship of economic resources, promoters of a world view and educators of the wider church. They must provide a continuing ecumenical context in which issues of worship, missionary and community policy and eucharistic sharing can be explored theologically and in other ways on behalf of the participating denominations.

LEPs are grit in the system, irritants capable of producing pearls of reconciliation and renewal.

Reconciliation will express the mutual acceptance of all members, ministries and sacraments in a form we cannot yet see in detail, but we are conscious that, as they are reconciled, the traditions of the churches will be reshaped by the kingdom to come, and unite the church in mission."

This handbook is intended to be an introduction to Local Ecumenical Partnerships in all their variety. In order to do this we have to set them in their context, and so we begin by taking up some of the questions around the nature of local ecumenism, what local ecumenical working makes possible, and the relation between local ecumenism and county and national bodies.

Biblical basis

There are many calls for unity in the Bible. Some of these are directed towards the whole created earth, others are more specifically directed towards the church. The call to unity is not a discovery of the mid to late 20th century. It is rooted in scripture and in the tradition of the church. It is rooted above all in the words of our Lord.

Jesus prayed for his followers: "May they all be one; as you, Father, are in me, and I am in you, so also may they be in us, that the world may believe that you sent me." (John 17:21 Revised English Bible). This prayer of Jesus, at the heart of the Gospel, underlies the search for Christian unity. If the church is to be obedient to the will of Our Lord, if it is to be a reflection of the life and community of the Holy Trinity, and if it is to have a concern for mission in all the world, then it needs also to look to its own life and what, in its life, it is witnessing to the world. The church is not witnessing to the reconciling power of God in Jesus Christ when it shows itself to the world outside to be divided. When the church grapples with fundamental and historic divisions in an endeavour to be reconciled, then it gains credibility in its witness to the world. In discovering diversity in its life the church can develop new models of living with variety in community.

General developments

The World Missionary Conference in Edinburgh in 1910 marked the start of the modern ecumenical movement. The search for unity has seen the forming of local Council of Churches (the first being in Bolton and Manchester in 1917), of the British Council of Churches in 1942, and of the World Council of Churches in 1948, bringing together different strands of the ecumenical movement. The Roman Catholic Church, while itself not being a member church of the World Council of Churches, has taken its own step along the ecumenical road, as in the Decree on Ecumenism in Vatican II in 1964, and more recently in the publication of the Ecumenical Directory (see bibliography).

The ecumenical movement internationally has seen a growth this century in bi-lateral and multi-lateral dialogues between the worldwide Christian communions. These are discussions that are happening between different Christian traditions about the issues that unite and divide, with a view to seeing whether churches can come closer together. A significant piece of ecumenical work of the World Council of Churches' Faith and Order Commission, of which the Roman Catholic Church is a full member, culminated in the publication of *"Baptism, Eucharist and Ministry"* (1982) (see bibliography). The convergences expressed in these documents provide the framework for much that is possible nationally and locally in Britain today.

Ecumenism in England – a change of emphasis from organic schemes to grass roots ecumenism

The post war years in England saw a growth of interest in schemes relating to the organic unity of the churches. There was a certain conviction that the way forward for church unity was for denominations to unite nationally. However, large schemes towards organic unity were on the whole unsuccessful. A scheme for union between the Church of England and the Methodist Church failed through an insufficient majority vote in the Church of England General Synod in 1972 as did the proposals for a covenant between the Methodist Church, the Moravian Church, the United Reformed Church and the Church of England in 1982. The Congregational Church and the Presbyterian Church in England came together to form the United Reformed Church in 1972. This new church united with the Churches of Christ in 1981. However, this unity scheme was not without its own difficulties: a number of Congregational churches stayed out of the URC and formed the Congregational Federation; the

4

Churches of Christ split and it was the Reformed Churches of Christ that entered into a union with the URC.

The post war decades also marked the rapid growth of secularisation and a growing uncertainty about the validity of ultimate truths. Different church traditions began to place more emphasis on their own sense of identity rather than on a renewed identity that would be found one with another.

The 80s, with its focus away from the welfare state and on the free market economy, helped to emphasise the need for consumer choice in many areas of life. Within the churches, this tendency led to a greater emphasis on the development of a variety of Christian traditions rather than on the desire for unity within and between different Christian traditions.

However, at the same time as the move away from the centralised state bureaucracy, there was a greater emphasis on the individual and to a certain extent on the local community. This development was paralleled in the church by a re-affirming of the grass roots, following the failure of the covenant proposals in 1982.

An emphasis on the local was there in England from the beginning of the ecumenical movement. The first local Councils of Churches were formed in Lancashire in 1917 and their numbers grew steadily during the rest of the century. After the Second World War new housing developments and the planning of new towns offered fresh opportunities for the churches to respond in different ways to the mission of the church. In 1964, the British Council of Churches Faith and Order Conference in Nottingham called for "areas of ecumenical experiment" to be established "at the request of local congregations, or in new towns and housing areas". The term "experiment" was used because it was hoped that in these areas the church authorities might allow them to go beyond the normal rules then applied by the churches, in the expectation that the churches would soon unite nationally. What began as experiments, however, came to be seen as having a life of their own. Hopes of national union schemes faded and churches began to amend their rules to allow for more ecumenical co-operation locally. The term "Local Ecumenical Project" was adopted in 1973 to describe what had formerly been designated "Areas of Ecumenical Experiment", and in 1995 "Project" was changed to "Partnership".

These local developments were followed in the 1980s by developments leading towards the formation of new national ecumenical bodies.

Ecumenical Instruments: An Introduction to the 1990 Ecumenical Structures

A new phase in ecumenical living in Britain and Ireland was inaugurated in September 1990, when the Inter Church Process *Not Strangers But Pilgrims* bore fruit in the establishment of new ecumenical structures for Britain and Ireland. This process expressed a change in approach to ecumenical theology and practice – a change which "requires a shift in thinking, feeling and action from ecumenism as an extra which absorbs energy, to ecumenism as a dimension of all that we do, which releases energy through the sharing of resources". The life of the British Council of Churches came to an end, and it was replaced by the new Council of Churches for Britain and Ireland (CCBI), and by national bodies in each of the four nations in these islands.

The CCBI includes a number of churches who were not full members of the British Council of Churches, for example the Roman Catholic Church in England and Wales and in Scotland, and brings together a wide variety of Christian traditions in Britain and Ireland. The CCBI seeks to co-ordinate and enable the life of the churches in such areas as public affairs, international affairs, church life, the community of women and men in the church and youth matters, and brings together those in the churches with responsibility for particular areas (in formal or informal networks). The CCBI provides a meeting place for the churches of the four nations where they can share concerns, talents and traditions in their calling to work together for unity in the church and in the world.

The churches deliberate together and formulate the agenda for the work of the CCBI at its bi-ennial Assembly, and the Church Representatives Meeting provides an opportunity for those designated and recognised by their own churches as representatives and leaders to meet together regularly for prayer, discussion and study, working together for the growth of visible unity and common mission in the life of the churches. The CCBI shares working accommodation at Inter-Church House in London with Christian Aid and with Churches Together in England, one of the three new national unity bodies established in 1990, the others being Action of Churches Together in Scotland (ACTS) and CYTUN (Churches Together in Wales), the successor to the Council of Churches for Wales.

Neither CCBI, CTE or CYTUN have large administrative structures, as they exist to facilitate the working and developing ecumenical life of the denominations, as the servants of the denominations, rather than to establish an additional ecumenical layer of church life. Those who represent the churches in these ecumenical instruments are people who are able to do so, and the authority of the ecumenical structures lies in the commitment of their member churches.

In England

Churches Together in England unites in pilgrimage those churches in England which "seek a deepening of their communion with Christ and with one another in the Church, which is his body" (CTE Constitution). CTE seeks to enable the churches in England to come to a common mind in their life and work together. The agenda for the work of CTE is shaped by the churches, reviewed every two years by the Forum, and is overseen and implemented by the Enabling Group which consists of officially appointed representatives of the denominations, together with regional representatives and those elected by the Forum. Churches Together in England brings together those from the churches concerned with specific issues in Co-ordinating Groups.

As well as enabling the ecumenical working of the churches at national level, Churches Together in England also has the task of relating to and supporting the life of the churches at intermediate level in counties, metropolitan areas and new towns. To facilitate this task Churches Together in England has two Field Officers, one for the midlands and north and one for the south of England.

Ecumenical relationships at the intermediate level are facilitated by "Churches Together" in counties, metropolitan areas or new towns. Before the changes in 1990, sponsoring bodies were already in existence in many areas, working to oversee and enable ecumenical living at the local level, particularly in the life and work of the Local Ecumenical Partnerships (in all their diverse forms, including local covenants). The present intermediate level bodies grew from these sponsoring bodies, from metropolitan area Councils of Churches, from developments in new towns, and also from the experience of other kinds of co-operative working at this level in, for example, local broadcasting, church leaders' meetings and industrial mission. The present intermediate bodies are varied in their forms and structures, reflecting the differing history and contexts in which they have developed.

An important part of the task of the intermediate level lies in facilitating community between levels, so that the ecumenical structures do not operate with an ecumenical imperative passing from the top down, but from an imperative which lies in the commitment of the participating churches at every level. The intermediate bodies help the churches to move from co-operation to commitment, and place the ecumenical issue on every agenda in each denomination. This is a move to a model of ecumenism which is internal to the life and structure of each local denomination, rather than being seen as an additional layer of activity external to the structures of the churches.

The agenda of the intermediate ecumenical bodies has expanded from that of the sponsoring bodies to include the support of all kinds of local ecumenical patterns and helping the churches at the intermediate level to think together about future planning, the deployment and sharing of resources, and decision making. The ecumenical instruments at the intermediate level also provide an opportunity for the churches to reflect together on the theological implications of their mutual commitment as well as working at the nuts and bolts of their relationship.

In Wales

The Council of Churches for Wales was established in 1956 and drew on the experience and commitment of The Welsh Ecumenical Society and the Joint Committee for Mutual Co-operation and Understanding between the Christian Communions in Wales (yes, that was its name!).

In the years leading up to 1956 and in the early life of the Council the primary concern was the search for unity in Wales. This led to a national faith and order conference in 1963 on the theme 'The unity we seek', (following the Montreal Conference of the WCC's Faith and Order Commission) which enabled the churches in Wales to reflect on their priorities in their search for Christian unity locally and nationally and prepared them for the seminal conference in Nottingham in 1964.

The result of these two events was a commitment by a number of the member churches of the Council to work together towards a covenant for union in Wales, which led to agreement by five of them in 1974 to covenant together towards visible union. The churches involved were the Church in Wales, the Methodist Church, the Presbyterian Church of Wales, the United Reformed Church and twelve congregations of the Baptist Union of Great Britain in South Wales. In 1976 the Commission of the Covenanted Churches was set up to foster the covenant locally and nationally. It has published a range of material to support this work including: a jointly authorised rite of Holy Communion (1981), a report on *Ministry in a Uniting Church* (1986), *Sharing Ministry* (1986), guidelines for LEPs in Wales, a baptismal service (1990), a report on *Christian Baptism and Church Membership* (1990) and a *Service of Affirmation and Reaffirmation of Faith* (1994). (See bibliography for details.)

Through the Council the churches were also able to develop a partnership in church and society issues. It made a significant contribution in a number of areas including the future of the Welsh language and culture, the role of the broadcasting media, governance and democracy in Wales, disarmament and peace, awareness-raising and action on apartheid in South Africa, and overseas aid and development. The Council developed considerable expertise in industrial and economic affairs through a series of consultations and publications and a highlight of this commitment was the denominations' joint action, through the council, during the dispute in the mining communities in 1984/5, which was regarded by many as *'the* sign of hope'.

Ecumenical collaboration in evangelism has not always been easy in Wales. In 1970 Wales for Christ was established by all the churches to develop a programme of training and evangelism primarily focused on the publication of the New Welsh Bible in three stages: the New Testament in 1975, the Psalms in 1979 and the whole Bible in 1988. The responsibility and resources of Wales for Christ have now been inherited by CYTUN's Commission on Evangelism.

From the very beginning Inter-Church Aid and now Christian Aid has played a crucial role in relation to aid and development. But in many villages and towns in Wales ecumenism began as a direct result of collaboration on Inter-Church Aid/Christian Aid. CYTUN is still able to draw on the experience and resources of Christian Aid as well as CAFOD in developing its work on justice and peace, environment and development, and worship and prayer.

The key ecumenical task in Wales, as elsewhere, is to ensure that these aspects of ecumenical commitment are held together in worship and mission locally and nationally.

CYTUN: Churches Together in Wales was established in 1990 as a successor to the Council of Churches for Wales (CCW). It shares its Basis and Commitment with the other national bodies and CCBI. It includes among its membership all those churches and denominations that were in membership of CCW, together with the Roman Catholic Church and the Religious Society of Friends. Only the 13 covenanted churches within the Baptist Union of Great Britain are in membership. The Lutheran Council of Great Britain, the Orthodox Churches and the Seventh Day Adventist Church are observers. Christian Aid, CAFOD and Christians against Torture are recognised as agencies, and there are 12 Bodies in Association.

Among its aims and priorities are: enabling the member churches and denominations to reflect together with a view to reaching a common mind and agreeing on common action; fostering local ecumenism (in collaboration with Enfys: The Commission of the Covenanted Churches, and the

Free Church Council of Wales); convening regular meetings of church leaders and chief executives; enabling specialist networks to contribute their experience and expertise, primarily through three commissions (see below); sharing information among the churches locally and nationally, mainly through CYTUN News, which is published about three times a year.

CYTUN functions through Y Gymanfa (The Assembly) which meets once every two years, the Council (meeting twice a year) and the Steering Committee (meeting four times a year). There are also three commissions: Ecumenical Affairs, Evangelism, and Wales and the World, which act as fora enabling those who bear responsibility for these areas of concern within their churches to share information and to agree common action.

CYTUN collaborates with other ecumenical agencies to support about 130 local CYTUN/Churches Together groups and 60 Local Ecumenical Projects [including a number of Gweinidogaethau Bro (Community ministries), primarily between the Welsh language non-conformist denominations].

2. WHAT IS A
LOCAL ECUMENICAL PARTNERSHIP?

One of the encouraging aspects of local ecumenism is that all Local Ecumenical Partnerships (LEPs) are different, and life in LEPs is always changing. This great diversity means that it is not possible to have a narrow definition of what an LEP is or is not. In this chapter we reflect in general terms on what can be seen as an LEP and some of the questions surrounding this. LEPs exist at the meeting point of mainstream denominations and yet are not seeking to be separate denominations. This leads, however, to a fluidity of life. The rich variety of local ecumenical experience is a matter for great rejoicing.

At the Swanwick Consultation on the future of Local Ecumenical Projects in March 1994, it was recommended that the title "Local Ecumenical Project" be changed to "Local Ecumenical Partnership". It was felt that this title gave a clearer indication of what was happening in local ecumenism and highlighted the way in which we were looking to partnerships between different Christian denominations rather than just between Christians from different traditions. The title "partnership" also conveys something of the pilgrimage element in local ecumenism – partnership is about growing and developing together in the faith while "project" may convey a more short term, one-off activity that could become separated from the main Christian traditions.

Definition

Local Ecumenical Partnership is defined as existing **"where there is a formal written agreement affecting the ministry, congregational life, buildings, and/or mission projects of more than one denomination; and a recognition of that agreement by the sponsoring body, and by the appropriate denominational authorities."** (Swanwick LEPs Consultation Report, March 1994). This agreement has to be ratified by the congregation(s) involved, the participating denominations and the sponsoring body.

The many different kinds of LEP, in their diversity of forms and situations, can be gathered under some general descriptions:

☆ **Covenant Partnership:** formal and solemn declaration in which local churches commit themselves to serve God together in their local situation. A local covenant is an agreement between a group of churches, often including the Roman Catholic Church to work and witness together, when possible, in a particular designated area. These covenants acknowledge the presence of different and separate congregations which, for denominational and historical reasons, have to remain distinct but have a commitment to share non-eucharistic worship, prayer and Bible study, and other aspects of church life and to share work within the wider community. *(See Chapter 3 (vi) for details on establishing a covenant partnership and the example of a local covenant in Appendix 3.)*

It should be noted that in local covenants, a variety of levels of involvement are possible between the different traditions within the covenant. It is possible within the local covenant to have churches which share eucharistic ministry and worship, alongside other traditions, in the same covenant, who are not able to participate as fully in the same way.

☆ **Church Partnership**: a formal and solemn declaration involving local churches in the following ways:

i. **Shared Building:** within the LEP there is at least one shared building, covered by a legal sharing agreement. This is not necessarily a church building; it could be a ministers house, a shop or a drop-in centre.

ii. **Shared Congregation:** there is considerable sharing of congregational life, probably involving worship, common life and witness, decision-making, pastoral care and perhaps finance.

iii. **Shared Ministry:** agreement has been reached for a shared sacramental ministry, which covers all sacramental services within the LEP, except marriages, which are covered by civil laws outside the control of the churches.

Editor's note: At the 1994 Consultation of LEPs the following four main categories of LEP were suggested. At the time of writing they have

12

not been agreed by member churches and a sub-committee of the Co-Ordinating Group for Local Unity is studying them.

"1.   Church Partnerships

 i A formal coming together of two or more existing congregations to share in their life and ministry.

 ii A church plant in a new area which from its inception is operated as a joint congregation with shared ministry.

 iii A shared building where there is a formal sharing agreement under the Sharing of Church Buildings Act.

 iv A church designated as a single church Local Ecumenical Partnership.

2. Covenant Partnerships
This category of partnership exists where a solemn written declaration has been made by two or more local churches, in which they pledge themselves to work in harmony and to do as much as possible together, and which has been registered with the Sponsoring Body.

3. Community Partnerships
This category covers a number of task orientated social responsibility projects where an agreement to operate ecumenically has been signed locally and is recognised by the Sponsoring Body.

4. Chaplaincy Partnerships
This category includes ministry orientated partnerships, such as prison, hospital, education, industry or other sector chaplaincies where an agreement to operate ecumenically has been signed locally and recognised by the Sponsoring Body."

Variety of local models

The following gives an indication of some of the variety of types and situations of LEPs. Detailed examples can be found in Chapter 3.

☆ **One congregation** comprising two or more denominations, meeting in one building and sharing worship life and ministry, for example on a new housing estate where several different denominations agree to share a building and worship; there will thus be one joint congregation in one shared building. Or in a more traditional area, where one church building is coming to the end of its life, the congregation may agree to share an established church building of another tradition; this agreement then moves toward the sharing of congregational life and ministry. Amongst the Free Churches, there are many examples of this happening, particularly in joint Baptist/United Reformed Churches or in joint Methodist/United Reformed Churches.

☆ **Two congregations** of different denominations, which may meet in one building and share certain aspects of their weekday life and ministry, but not their Sunday worship, for instance in an Anglican parish church where there is an Anglican service at 9.30am and a Free Church service at 11.00am. Although Sunday worship is separate, there can be an agreement to work and share together wherever possible during the week. A pattern of regular united worship on agreed Sundays throughout the year may also develop.

☆ **A group of congregations** of different denominations in an area, which commit themselves to working together but continue with their own individual Sunday worship patterns. The shared ministry in such an area can often lead to the development of a good team ministry.

☆ **A shared parish**, where the local churches of different denominations in one parish agree to share worship and ministry while still retaining separate buildings. This can lead to a renewal of the worship life of all the congregations in the area, as they come to experience more of the different traditions.

☆ **A town centre,** where there can be an agreement amongst all the churches in that area to look again at what town centre ministry is about and to develop this. This can lead to shared projects while the worshipping congregations still remain separate.

☆ **A rural area,** where pressures often build up because of the lack of full time ordained ministry. There can be a real possibility for sharing in ministry over several villages so that between the denominations, the needs of each village are met; the single church LEP is a growing development in rural areas. This raises the question of cross authorisation of ministries – could it be envisaged that one day there

14

could be an agreement to have an Anglican vicar in one village who serves both Free Churches and Anglicans in that village, and a Methodist minister in a neighbouring village who serves both Anglicans and Methodists in that village?

The type of written agreement necessary varies from place to place. Where one building is shared by more than one denomination, it is essential to have a sharing agreement. Where a group of local churches are co-operating across an area but retaining their separate identities and building, it is usual to have a covenant. When congregational life or ministry are shared, it is normal to have a constitution. In some places, all three agreements will be present, for instance a building that is shared by an Anglican/Free Church congregation and a Roman Catholic congregation will have a sharing agreement defining the ownership of the building, a covenant defining the commitment between the Anglican Free Church congregation and the Roman Catholic congregation, and a constitution defining the way the life of the church works out in practice (*for detailed guidance see bibliography*).

Other forms of ecumenical partnership

☆ **Prisons.** Prison Chaplaincy is often the basis for a good ecumenical team. While there are statutory requirements for denominational chaplains working in prisons for the Church of England, the Methodist Church and the Roman Catholic Church, it is possible for those so appointed in this way to commit themselves to shared work in any one prison.

☆ **Universities.** Chaplaincies in institutions of higher and further education can also be formally constituted as LEPs. In these cases, it needs to be clear as to who is actually entering and agreeing the LEP status at the local level, as the "congregational" element changes year by year. In some cases representatives of the institution are signatories to the agreement. The intermediate body will normally be the appropriate sponsoring body.

☆ **Hospitals.** Many hospital chaplaincies have good ecumenical working relationships and, in a number of places where these have become well established, there are formal ecumenical partnerships known as "hospital chaplaincy covenants". It is important, however, to realise that hospital chaplains, both part time and whole time, have dual accountability. They have an accountability to the NHS Trust or other health authority which employs them as chaplains, and also to the denomination which authorises their ministry.

A hospital chaplaincy covenant is a covenant within the chaplaincy and between all the chaplains, approved and endorsed by, on the one hand, the employing NHS Trust/other health authority and, on the other hand, the nominating bodies. The nominating bodies for hospital chaplaincy are the appropriate diocese, represented by the bishop for Anglican and Roman Catholic chaplains, and the national Free Church Federal Council for the Free Churches.

It is probably appropriate that a hospital chaplaincy covenant should be registered with the relevant intermediate ecumenical sponsoring body. However, it must be realised that the sponsoring body cannot expect to have oversight of these covenants in the same way as it does over most LEPs, since the chaplains are appointed and employed by the NHS Trust/other health authority and not by the denominations.

The Churches Committee for Hospital Chaplaincy, a co-ordinating group of Churches Together in England, is in the process of producing advisory notes which will be available to hospital chaplaincies wishing to consider a hospital chaplaincy covenant.

☆ **Local Radio, Industrial Mission, Christian Training Courses and Joint Work in Social Responsibility** may also be the focus for local ecumenical partnerships.

Variety of denominational involvement

LEPs are places where more than one Christian tradition shares together in some form of life, worship, work and witness and where there is a common agreement to enable this sharing to happen. This means that, denominationally, LEPs can be very varied. They normally include one of the following:-

i. Any combination of the Free Churches on their own;
ii. A combination of Free Churches and the Church of England;
iii. A combination of Free Churches, the Church of England and the Roman Catholic Church;
iv. The Church of England and the Roman Catholic Church.

Other churches that are sometimes also involved include:

16

The Salvation Army,
The Quakers,
Black-Majority Churches,
Independent or new House Churches,
Orthodox Churches,
Lutheran Churches.
The Moravian Church

The variety of denominations involved will determine the kind of agreement that is to be entered in to, as different denominations permit different things to happen.

It should be noted that different things are possible as different denominations co-operate together. The following are examples:-

- when different Free Churches work together, it is possible to have a fully shared ministry;
- when the Church of England is involved, sacramental sharing is permissible (including joint confirmation) and some shared ministry is allowed under Canon B44 (*see Appendix 4*), but ministry is not fully interchangeable with other traditions;
- when the Roman Catholic Church is involved, general eucharistic sharing is not permissible, but there have been significant local developments involving the Roman Catholic Church over the last two decades such as the growing participation of the Roman Catholic Church in local covenants and shared buildings.

Living with our histories

Historic divisions in the churches, which have been in place for centuries, are not resolved overnight. It is helpful to have an understanding of the history of our traditions in order to see the limits of possibilities within an LEP. If an LEP is not to become either separated from the historic denominations or a new denomination, it has to take seriously the legacies of the past. However, these constraints can be seen as possibilities – and an exploration of perceived constraints can be enriching. In studying and understanding the matters which have traditionally divided the churches over the centuries, there can be a renewed grasp of those things which are central to the faith and which we can all share. It is also interesting to reflect on the ways in which social, economic and political factors have been bound up with perceived theological differences in the different traditions. [Note: The self-understanding of each denomination with regard to theology and practice varies. Each denomination has been asked to make

17

a contribution to this handbook about its own self-understanding with regard to theology and practice. *(See Appendix I)*]

Short courses in the matters that are, and have been, significant to each of our different Christian traditions can be a helpful way of proceeding to develop an understanding of our differences. These can happen in a fairly informal way. A number of people, either lay or ordained, representing their different traditions, can speak about what their tradition means to them and be asked to touch briefly on the historic background of the contemporary understanding. Such short courses can be mounted on an informal basis within any one LEP, or can be mounted across a town or a wider area, where resources from existing denominational churches can be shared for the benefit of all.

Some Advantages and Challenges of Local Ecumenism

i. **Deepening faith from an understanding of different traditions.** Coming closer to people from different traditions gives an opportunity to deepen our own Christian faith. As we learn why areas of faith and practice have been important for people in other denominations, so it is possible for our own faith to be deepened and our own practice of the Christian life to be broadened. This can happen in a whole variety of ways, to be discovered anew in each LEP:

    ●   The first time someone witnesses a baptism by immersion can be a deeply moving experience that evokes a personal renewal of faith.

    ●   Entering into the devotion of the Stations of the Cross can lead to a deepening experience of the reality of our Lord's Passion.

    ●   Sharing together in a weekly Eucharist rather than once a month or once a quarter can be an enriching experience and can give a new opportunity for a deeper reflection on the death of Christ for all the world.

    ●   Freer forms of worship can be seen as a cutting edge of mission, as they lead the church to be more accessible to those who are not used to church-going.

    ●   Different forms of oversight, authority and decision-making can lead to a renewed understanding of both the New Testament church and the historic tradition of the church. On the one hand, congregational decision-making can help to deepen understanding of the participation of lay people in the life of the church. On the other hand, episcopal oversight can foster a growing awareness of the wider unity and continuity of the church. The Methodist circuit system is sometimes seen as a model for local ecumenical development, when a number of congregations come together in one area to share a common life and to share in a common ministry.

ii.   **A model for reconciliation.** In a world that is perceived as increasingly divided on a national and international scale and in which interpersonal relationships are sometimes seen as increasingly difficult, LEPs offer the possibility of new models of reconciliation. As a local community has to grapple with issues which have been divisive during the history of the church and yet is able to work positively with these issues to create renewed communities, so LEPs can offer new possibilities of hope. This can happen, for instance, in an LEP which is able to come to a working agreement about such matters as the question of baptism, or the reservation of the blessed sacrament for Roman Catholics, where the LEP involves traditions which have a variety of different beliefs and practices in these two areas. This means not only looking at the theological issues involved, but also looking at ways of working in which strongly held differing views can be drawn together in creatively. In many LEPs, what unites is discovered to be much stronger that what has historically divided.

iii. **Isolation and networking.** When an LEP is established in isolation from other LEPs, problems can arise through the lack of a wider support network for that LEP. Those at the grass roots can feel that they are on their own facing the questions that come to them. It is helpful to be in touch with others who share similar experiences, in order both to gain support and not to re-invent the wheel. Systems of support can be developed through the work of the sponsoring body for the area. There are also, from time to time, opportunities for sharing and training at intermediate, regional and national levels.

iv.   **Increasing meetings.** It sometimes seems that the growth of ecumenism has more to do with the growth in the number of meetings than anything else, and it is true that, when embarking on the ecumenical journey, the number of meetings always increases in the short term. Inevitably, it takes time to reach agreement and understanding between people of different traditions. However this stage should not continue forever. As the churches grow in understanding, they should be able to work closely together, and this may well include the replacement of parallel denominational groups and meetings by joint ones.

v. **Is being ecumenical only a response to the need to be economical?** Sometimes it seems that it is necessary to be ecumenical for economical reasons – it is cheaper to share church buildings, it saves on person power to share ministry. When building new churches on a new housing estate, it is certainly cheaper to build one than to build three or four in a row. It can be argued that it is a better use of resources, but this will not be the only reason for embarking on this course of action.

vi. **Are LEPs new denominations?** It is sometimes said that Local Ecumenical Partnerships are pre-empting national unity schemes by forming new denominations of their own. Some people fear that traditional denominational patterns are not able to be recognised in any one LEP. However, this begs the question of whether, within any one denomination, each local congregation exactly reflects the same denominational practice, or whether there is not some flexibility within each of the main Christian traditions. The development of local ecumenism raises the question, faced by all our traditions, of the appropriate ways in which the local church belongs to the wider church.

LEPs do always in fact belong to their parent denominations. The fact that an LEP is defined by having a written agreement approved by the participating denominations makes it clear that the formal link with the denominations is retained. It is not possible to constitute an LEP without the assent of the denominations involved. It is useful for an LEP to look at itself and see whether it has recognisable elements from its partner traditions readily visible in its life. This does at times mean engaging in study about the recognisable elements in each of the participating traditions. It is also important for the denominations involved and the LEP to establish a good, ongoing, working relationship, in order to sustain the sense of the LEP belonging to the different denominations, and vice versa (*see also Chapter 6: Working Towards Unity*). So LEPs are not new denominations; they are local experiences of the given unity of the churches.

vii. **Liberal or evangelical: theological uniformity?** It is sometimes argued that the ecumenical movement has overemphasised catholicity and endeavoured to embrace a wide range of theological perspectives without actually addressing "truth" questions with regard to the Christian faith. There is instead an emphasis on the need for a growth in mutual understanding, when people of two or more different traditions come together.

Being ecumenical is sometimes seen as being at the opposite end of the spectrum to being evangelical, or being Pentecostal, or being independent. There are also times when it feels as if ecumenism works against evangelism, because of the amount of time that needs to be taken in order to develop mutual understanding between different traditions.

However, one of the strands of the ecumenical journey is the renewal of the churches for mission in its widest sense. Just as LEPs have the possibility of developing new understandings from differing Christian traditions, so may they also draw from different theological perspectives. Thus, it is possible in an LEP for the perceived dividing lines between such perspectives as liberal and evangelical to be crossed to their mutual benefit and new theological insights about the Christian faith to be gained by both. This can, in fact, offer a new model of working to the major Christian traditions where these theological emphases are sometimes just as divisive.

Engaging together in evangelism can often appeal to people outside the church, who find difficulties with what they perceive as inter-church wrangling. It also gets round the "escape clause" sometimes used by nominal Christians who claim to belong to another denomination than that of the Christian who visits them.

3. HOW TO SET UP AN LEP

Each Local Ecumenical Partnership represents churches moving from co-operation to commitment in a particular local context, and partnerships are shaped not only by the participating denominations but by their local situation, by the particular human community which they serve.

An LEP is not the beginning of local commitment, but the expression of local commitment; nor is it the end result of local commitment, as the partnership is there to enable ecumenical relationships to continue to develop, both between those churches that make up the LEP, and with other Christian communities in the area who are not part of the formal relationship at its inauguration. LEPs are called to be ecumenical instruments, enabling all kinds of relationships in their local situation. It is important that LEPs are conscious of the possibility that they may deepen their relationship with one another at the expense of a broader spread of relationships with other churches. The partnership should remain open to the possibility of other churches joining in the future, and be open to working with them in informal ways in the meantime.

Getting Started

In the beginning someone is brave enough to make the first move with the suggestion that the existing good relationship between Christian communities in a particular place should be recognised in a formal commitment to one another and to God. This first move might be made by anyone locally, or sometimes it might be the county or denominational ecumenical officer who asks whether this might be an appropriate next step. At this point the potential for development needs to be as open as possible, and those involved locally need to get as much information as they can about what is feasible and what is not. It can be helpful to invite the ecumenical officer to come and discuss the situation at this stage, and he or she will be able to suggest other LEPs in similar kinds of contexts. These could be visited by those involved locally, so that they can see how things are on the ground, and hear both the positive and negative sides of the experience. This initial phase of consultation needs to be as wide as possible, and it is important that everyone involved is kept well informed. Those involved locally should talk to the ministers and leaders of other local churches or possible partners in the LEP to find out whether they are interested, making sure that they are kept informed even if they decide not to join at this stage. The most important part of this initial and all subsequent phases in the development of an LEP is that everyone is able to feel that they have the information they need, and that their opinion of what is proposed has been heard.

Local Ecumenical Partnerships in practice

The Village

This LEP is a single church in a small rural community and is based on very long-term relationships between two Christian communities. The congregations know one another well and had an expectation of working together which was expressed in a local covenant three years ago. When the Methodist church discovered last year that their building was in need of extensive repairs, it seemed natural for the two communities to move into one building. A sharing agreement was prepared for the parish church, and the local covenant was re-drawn to embrace the new situation; on Easter Day the two communities became one ecumenical congregation. Those from the Methodist church made up one third of the total congregation, and the two communities engaged in a careful discussion about how the worship and life of the new congregation would reflect the contributions of both traditions. The new congregation uses the Methodist hymnbook "Hymns and Psalms", and is part of the Methodist Circuit Preaching Plan, so that the vicar gives three appointments a quarter to the circuit and Methodist local preachers come regularly to take part in worship. The Methodist minister who has pastoral charge is involved in leading worship and in the life of the congregation. On the third Sunday in the month, Morning Prayer has become a Methodist morning service, and Holy Communion on the fifth Sunday is a Methodist communion service with distribution in individual cups. There is one church council, and the ecumenical congregation is represented on both the Anglican Deanery Synod and the Methodist Circuit Meeting. Local people describe a renewed sense of purpose in fulfilling their vocation together to be God's people in this village. Questions arise over how they can work with the parish church in the other village within the Anglican benefice, and with Roman Catholics and Baptists who live in the village but travel to the nearby town for their church life.

In Wales

In Wales there will be communities where worship is available in Welsh or English or in a combination of both. This can complicate attempts at collaboration, but a solution has been found to group churches in language families.

The New Housing Estate

This LEP began not with developed local relationships but with an almost blank sheet of paper. Five years ago, representatives of the churches met with one another and with planning officers and developers and agreed on one building to serve the needs of the new community. This multi-purpose building would be located alongside other community facilities, including First and Middle Schools, shops and a doctors surgery and situated on a level site. Two years later the first minister, from the United Reformed Church, was appointed jointly by the denominations. He and his family were among the first people to move in, and he began by gathering a few Christians, whom he met through involvement in the embryonic community, to worship in his house. Among these were three Methodists from an adjoining estate, who had been travelling some distance to worship, but who now committed themselves to support the new church. A constitution was prepared for the new church which was flexible enough to cover them over a period of change and development; gradually people moved in to the new houses, mud became roads, the schools were opened and the growing congregation began to meet for worship in the school hall. Two years later, when there were thirty people meeting regularly, funding arrangements had been agreed and a sharing agreement prepared, the denominations gave the 'go ahead' to begin construction of the new building. It now provides a home for community groups during the week and for a Seventh Day Adventist Church on Saturdays. A Roman Catholic congregation worships in the building at 9am on Sundays, before the ecumenical congregation meets for worship at 10.30am. Sometimes the congregations share coffee between the services and they also have occasional shared worship at festivals and a joint Christmas card which goes to the whole local area with details of all the Christmas services.

The Market Town

In this market town there was a Council of Churches which flourished for twenty years doing the things that Councils of Churches often do – Christian Aid Week, Lent Groups, a Good Friday March of Witness, social events and visiting speakers. There was sometimes a sense of people

coming along just to support the events, but on the whole good relation-
ships were established between the churches. In 1990 the introduction of
new national ecumenical instruments meant that Roman Catholics became
more deeply involved, and they brought a fresh enthusiasm for the ecu-
menical task. The Council of Churches became Churches Together and
undertook an audit of their resources in people and buildings and of the
needs of the town. The audit prompted the churches to begin to run an after
school club and a school holiday play scheme. The Churches Together
decided to ask the Christian Fellowship and the Anglicans to undertake
youth work on behalf of the other churches. The churches found that they
experienced a growing sense of commitment as they got to know one
another through these shared projects, and two years after the change of
structure they decided to make a local covenant, to express their relation-
ship and their hope that it would continue to deepen. This local covenant
embraces nine congregations from seven denominations – Baptists,
Methodists, Anglicans, Roman Catholics, Christian Fellowship, Religious
Society of Friends and Salvation Army. The focus of their inter-relation-
ship is on mission and service to the town, and they continue some of the
former activities of the Council of Churches. This kind of LEP is repeated
in differing forms and with differing combinations of denominations: in
Wales it might include the Union of Welsh Independents and the
Presbyterian Church of Wales.

Local Ecumenical Partnerships have also been established in Prison and
College Chaplaincies, in Industrial Mission Christian Training Courses, in
inner city contexts where the churches might otherwise have had to with-
draw from the area and in a huge range of other community and chaplaincy situations. There are many other possible models for developing
LEPs, and from the examples above it can be seen that people begin to set
up LEPs in a wide variety of situations. The decision to move from co
-operation to commitment is always part of a continuing process, although
it is easier to see this process when the formation of the LEP involves
existing congregations moving to deepen their relationship. In the example of the new estate the existing relationship is between the denominations at the level of the intermediate body, acting as sponsoring body,
and church leaders.

An LEP is a commitment by the whole church: not only the local congregation but the rest of their denomination, who must give approval to the
form of local involvement through their structures for decision making.
Whatever form of commitment is proposed, it is important that churches
do not move forward to make a commitment to one another if a large

26

proportion of those involved locally are unsure; it is better to spend more time in preparation for the establishment of the project than to move forward on a limited commitment. The partnership cannot be built only on the enthusiasm of a few people, but must express the vision and hopes of a majority of those involved locally.

Moving on

Those involved in the local situation now move into the next stage of the conversation, in consultation with the denominational authorities who need to think through the implications for ministry, finance, planning, resources, and buildings, and who will help with the theological implications as well as the practical ones. These might arise in the areas of worship, structures for church government, different polity and sources of authority, styles of mission, concepts of the church, membership, sacraments, re-marriage of divorced people and religious language and meaning, to mention only a few. This theological exploration of the ground rules is not a search for problems, but a recognition that there are differences between the denominations, and the implications for each local situation need to be carefully considered.

The next stage in the establishment of the LEP is the preparation of a suitable "declaration of intent" and constitution.

Declarations of Intent and Constitutions for Local Ecumenical Partnerships

i.   Why do we need a Constitution?

There is sometimes resistance to drawing up constitutions, and they can prove difficult to formulate where there is a complicated local situation; however the document exists first and foremost to enable the life and work of the LEP. The constitution is designed to accommodate the needs of the denominations in this local situation, as far as possible, and begins with a "declaration of intent" for the future life of the partnership. This declaration helps to define the project; from this definition comes the formulating of appropriate structures to support and enable the life of the project, safeguarding the underlying theological principles of the participating denominations (for example over baptism, initiation and membership). The constitution makes clear the expectations the local church has of the intermediate body or of the sponsoring body, and of the denominations.

ii. Where to go for help and advice

County or denominational ecumenical officers will work with the local church and liaise with sponsoring denominations over the initial drafts, so that time and effort are not wasted. Denominational ecumenical officers will also be able to offer any denominationally specific information that is required. It is often helpful to begin with one of the draft outlines suggested, in order to avoid re-invention of the wheel. For names and addresses of county ecumenical officers contact Churches Together in England *(see Appendix 8)*, and relevant church headquarters for denominational ecumenical officers.

iii. The Declaration of Intent

This is a brief statement which outlines the agreed theological basis for working together, and the nature and purpose of the covenant commitment which is being entered into *(see Appendix 3)*. The declaration of intent often forms the focal point for the act of worship which inaugurates the LEP. If the partnership is in a specialised context, for example in a prison or school chaplaincy, then the declaration of intent needs to be drawn up to embrace and describe the particular circumstances.

iv. The Constitution

The constitution should be based on the nationally agreed guidelines (*see bibliography*), but should also reflect the local situation, as this forms the distinctive character of LEPs almost as much as the participating denominations.

If the LEP will be sharing buildings, it is important to make sure that a joint council, established according to the constitution, is included in the sharing agreement as specified by the *Sharing of Church Buildings Act 1969*. The sharing agreement is a legal document, and is separate from the LEP constitution (see Chapter 4 and also *Under the Same Roof: Guidelines to the Sharing of Church Buildings Act 1969*, CTE 1994).

v. Is everyone agreed?

☆ **The Local Church.** The constitution will probably be drafted by a small group consisting of perhaps the minister, elders, deacons or church wardens or others to whom the task is given. The declaration of intent and constitution must reflect the intention of the wider congregation, and it is helpful if those drafting are careful about the process of explanation, accepting suggestions and ideas before a final draft is produced. This may be brought to the Church Meeting for approval, especially if the proposed LEP involves the coming together of a number of existing congregations, so that the partnership begins with as great a sense of unity of purpose as possible.

☆ **The Sponsoring Body.** The constitution should have been drafted in consultation with the intermediate body or sponsoring body, the County Ecumenical Officer, or sub-group of the intermediate body responsible for this area. This pattern of consultation reduces the chance of the constitution being rejected at this point, which can be a difficult experience for local churches who have put a lot of work in to the draft. Apart from the approval of the representatives on behalf of their denominations, the intermediate body also has to approve the constitution on its own behalf because it will make demands on the intermediate body in terms of support and review.

☆ **The Participating Denominations.** Although the intermediate body is constituted of representatives of the denominations, the proposed constitution must still be referred to the appropriate structures for regulating ecumenical relationships in the denominations. In some denominations this will be a national ecumenical officer, in others it may be the diocesan bishop or a committee at the intermediate level. Sometimes these denominational people, who see many LEP constitutions, are able to make helpful suggestions about any remaining points of difficulty. It is important that the LEP is seen to be established with the proper authority of the sponsoring denominations. This both makes the exercise legal or officially approved, and therefore enables inter-church living to develop within the LEP in ways which would not be permissable elsewhere, and also helps those participating in the local commitment to remain part of the wider church, as represented by their denominations. The local commitment is made in the context of the universality of the church.

vi. Covenant Partnerships

Those involved locally contemplating a local covenant should similarly seek advice over their draft covenant, which is often the same kind of document as the declaration of intent for a more tightly drawn LEP, but should be drawn to reflect the local situation. It is useful for local covenants to have a suitable and agreed constitution to ensure that appropriate structures are in place to enable the working of the covenant.

In situations where the covenant embraces a local Churches Together group which has developed from a local Council of Churches there may be quite a large number of member churches. In these cases the CTE draft constitution for Churches Together or examples available from CYTUN, may be useful plus a formal declaration of intent for the covenanted relationship.

"The fact that covenanting is performed with the approval of those in authority and is concerned with definite activities shows the inter-relationship of church leaders and congregations. Without the leaders a covenant would have no authority; without the congregations' activities it would have no substance." (From 'Local Churches in Covenant', Roman Catholic Bishops in England and Wales.)

vii. Celebrating Commitment

Local Ecumenical Partnerships should be inaugurated in a public and celebratory way, at a service attended by representatives of the local church and the intermediate or sponsoring body and church leaders, who are all seen to give official support and encouragement to the local commitment being entered into.

viii. Reviewing and Renewing Commitment

Procedures for changing and adapting the constitution need to be agreed with the intermediate body, and it is generally better not to put into the constitution things that might need to change and evolve, especially in new projects. It is helpful to agree policy on certain things when the partnership is initiated – for example styles of worship and ministerial responsibilities, but what need to be protected by being outlined in the constitution are principles rather than details.

It is usually stated that the constitution is for a set period, five or seven years, after which the life of the LEP is reviewed, the constitution may be revised if necessary and the LEP is re-designated by the intermediate body for a further period. The declaration of intent can be useful as a measure for development and as a record of the founding vision of the project in this process of review (see Chapter 5 for more details on reviews of LEPs).

4. LIFE IN AN LEP

Life in an LEP is experienced in a variety of ways. LEPs are shaped by the different contexts in which they find themselves and the different denominations which are involved.

This chapter is by no means an exhaustive list of what can be done together but looks at some of the more complex issues which arise when people of different traditions join together. This means that many areas which make up the life of an LEP are not covered, for instance social and community action, or mission and evangelism. This is not because these aspects of life are not integral to each LEP, but rather because this chapter looks at areas which are specific to LEPs and are often at the forefront when an LEP is being established or developing its work.

This chapter is particularly looking at LEPs who are already experiencing, or wanting to experience, shared congregational life, team ministries, or shared staffing. It also covers questions about how decisions are reached and touches on some matters to do with the sharing of property. These are all areas where we differ denominationally to a greater or lesser extent. This chapter explores some ways in which it is possible to work together.

Worship

Worship can be a matter in which our differences are most clearly focused and seem to be most hard to reconcile. It can also be the most renewing experience for the life of any one local church and the main way in which people are brought together in a deepening unity.

i. Questions and possibilities

Many questions arise when congregations of two or more traditions first encounter one another and begin to compare notes on their current worship practices. hese practices are often sensitive because they have shaped denominational identity. Below are outlined some of the questions which may be raised and an indication of a few of the responses that it is possible to make in an LEP.

31

Should there be individual cups or one chalice at Communion?
In an LEP it is possible to decide to have one or the other, or to alternate the practice on successive Sundays, or to offer people the choice at the same service.

Should there be alcoholic, de-alcoholised, or non-fermented wine?
In an LEP there can be an interesting discussion on the use of different kinds of wine and the background to this use. In some LEPs people have decided to use one kind of wine or the other; in other LEPs, both kinds of wine are available.

Should people stay in their seats or come forward to receive Communion?
This question can lead to a useful discussion about the different principles underlying why some traditions remain in their seats and others move forward. In an LEP it is possible to alternate practices or, by common agreement, to decide on one practice or another.

Should wafers or bread be used?
This question opens up the possibility of discussing our different practices and customs and their historical origins before coming to a consensus as to local practice.

Should communion be daily/weekly/monthly/or quarterly?
In differing LEPs it is possible to have differing patterns. In some, weekly communion will be the norm, in others fortnightly. In some there will be an earlier communion service and a later non-eucharistic service each Sunday morning.

What about the hymn book? Should it be of one denomination or another? Should it be a new, modern hymn book? Should it contain more traditional hymns? Should a book be dispensed with and an overhead projector used?
Some LEPs opt for a hymn book of another country's Uniting Church, eg. With One Voice from the Australian Uniting Church. Other LEPs with a more informal approach will use an overhead projector. For some LEPs the forming of the partnership is an opportunity to buy a new hymn book; for others it is an opportunity to experience alternately the hymn books of the participating traditions.

What about the liturgy? Should it be printed out, the same each week, or not printed out but developed spontaneously?

32

In LEPs it is possible for the practice to vary. However, it should be noted that the adoption of regular eucharistic or baptismal liturgies can need formal denominational approval .

Should there be a rotation of services from the different traditions or the development of new, ecumenical services?
In some LEPs new work is done on developing patterns of worship. In others there is a rotation week by week of services from the different traditions.

What about musical accompaniment? Organ / piano / guitars / the voice alone?
In LEPs, as in one denominational congregations, the answer to this question often depends on the variety of gifts available within the congregation.

What about the length of the sermon? Five, ten or twenty minutes, or half an hour?
A useful discussion can be held in LEPs about the role of the sermon in our different traditions, as well as a review of effective ways of communicating the Gospel.

Who will lead the service? Should more than one tradition participate in the leading of worship each Sunday? Should there be leadership by more than one tradition on a rotating basis across several weeks? Is it sufficient for one person, of one tradition, to be authorised to be the regular leader of worship in an ecumenical congregation?
In some LEPs, one person of one tradition will be authorised to be the regular leader of worship. However it is helpful to have people of the other traditions represented in that LEP sharing in the leading of worship, if only from time to time. The formation of local worship teams from members of the congregation can be a helpful asset.

Different problems arise for one-denominational congregations, sharing in partnership with other churches up the road. How do they come to experience the richness and variety of worship that is possible across the traditions?
It is possible to develop a programme of shared worship where from time to time visits are made to other churches in the same partnership in the area. Shared worship does not necessarily mean developing new ecumenical services, it can mean sharing as fully as possible in the services offered within one particular denominational tradition.

While some of these questions are specifically ecumenical ones, others are to be found within any one of our Christian traditions. When these questions arise, it is important to take time to consider the views underlying the questions. Often, personal preferences and many non-theological factors will be involved in views about appropriate forms of worship. These are not questions to which there is necessarily one answer and local practice may vary.

While there are many questions that need discussing in LEPs, it is also true that there are many possibilities of renewed and varying ways of worship that can be enriching to a congregation. As the congregation comes to experience something of the wealth of what each tradition has to offer, so its own worship life can be developed and enhanced.

Worshipping in an LEP can give increased access to the growing variety of worship material that is available across our traditions. Material from any one tradition can be used by a variety of traditions coming together in an LEP, thus enhancing the worship of that LEP. The Liturgical Renewal Movement within the Roman Catholic Church has much to offer. Worship material from places further afield, such as Iona, Taizé, the charismatic renewal movements, and the World Council of Churches, can also be a source of enrichment.

ii. Eucharistic worship

What is permissible with regard to the Eucharist varies, depending on the traditions involved in an ecumenical partnership. If only Free Churches are involved, there is a greater flexibility with regard to interchangeability of ministry and the drawing up of new orders of service.

When the Free Churches and the Church of England are involved together, Canon B44 of the Church of England permits a certain degree of interchangeability of ministry (*see Appendix 4*). It is possible to have a shared Anglican/Free Church congregation in which those who are ordained within any of these traditions may preside at Holy Communion in rotation. The question then arises of which liturgy to use. There are three different possibilities here:-

- to use the denominational liturgies in rotation week by week.
- to use internationally agreed liturgies, e.g. Lima *(see bibliography)* or new British liturgies such as those produced by the Iona Community
- to draw up new local liturgies.

However, if the second or third option is chosen the appropriate authorisation of each participating denomination and the sponsoring body are needed. Both the drawing up of a new order of service and the gaining of authorisation for it can be a time consuming process, but the process itself can help the congregation understand the meaning of the liturgy, and authorisation is necessary for the LEP to continue within the traditions of the separate participating denominations.

The involvement of the Roman Catholic Church in an ecumenical partnership presents other possibilities. Variations in the self-understanding of different traditions mean that sharing the eucharistic elements with Roman Catholics is not permissible. However, there are many other ways to share together. It is possible for Roman Catholics coming to Anglican/Free Church services of Holy Communion, or members of the Church of England and the Free Churches going to Roman Catholic Mass, to go forward to receive a blessing from the presiding minister or priest. The pain caused by our not being able to receive communion together can encourage and goad people to work harder in the search for unity.

iii. Non-eucharistic worship

There are many possibilities of sharing together across all our traditions in non-eucharistic services. Special occasions, such as the Week of Prayer for Christian Unity; celebrations of the work of Christian Aid or CAFOD (the Catholic overseas development agency); or Prayers for Peace can lead to a sharing across the different traditions. It is also possible in a local partnership, such as a local covenant, to have a regular agreed pattern of evening services that are non-eucharistic, enabling a variety of ways of worship to be experienced, such as meditation, bible study, liturgical dance and different forms of music. Regular lunchtime services during the week is also an option as are prayer groups which can be a very enriching experience for the people of different traditions involved.

The appointment of staff to Local Ecumenical Partnerships

The appointment of new staff members in LEPs can be crucial to their well-being and further development. It is important that the intermediate body, in its role as sponsoring body, is able to offer support and advice within the various appointment procedures of the denominations involved, through an agreed policy on appointments. Alongside this policy, it is good practice for the intermediate body to establish guidelines for situations where relationships between staff and the LEP or sponsoring denominations break down for any reason. Normally the denomination which is responsible for making the appointment would expect to follow its usual appointments procedure, with the addition of appropriate ecumenical consultation, as outlined below. In LEPs where a single minister is appointed to work on behalf of all the participating denominations, this consultation is of even greater importance. In such situations, the intermediate body should be prepared to look well ahead in planning new appointments, as making the appointment can prove a lengthy process.

i. Some suggested guidelines for good practice in appointments

☆ The intermediate body should have an **agreed procedure** for the appointment of clergy and ministers to Local Ecumenical Partnerships. Recognising that a wide range of ecumenical developments will be represented in any area, those responsible for appointments in the denominations and those in local situations are asked to act flexibly within these guidelines, in response to particular local contexts.

☆ It is vital for the continuing development of LEPs that clergy and ministers appointed to any church within them are **fully committed** to their aims. The final right of appointment remains with the denomination concerned, and the appointment will be made according to its usual appointments' procedure. However there should be the fullest and earliest co-operation and consultation between those making the appointment and the other partners in the LEP.

☆ Consultation may take place through the medium of a **staffing consultative group**, established by the intermediate body, the support group, local advisory group or consultant or link-person and the project. The staffing consultative group consists of local lay and ministerial representatives from all the participating denominations, representatives of the intermediate body and the appropriate representatives from the structures of the denominations, for example circuit stewards and the bishop or his nominee. If a staffing consultative group is appointed, then it should be involved in drawing up or revising the job description, which is then sent to the appointing denomination and to the intermediate body and the other participating denominations. The staffing consultative group does not make the appointment, but is able to offer authoritative advice to those who do. The group should therefore have an opportunity to meet candidates at an early point in the process, so that ecumenical consultation plays a significant part in the final decision.

☆ If the intermediate body does not use a staffing consultative group, then it is still important that **consultation on the appointment** with existing clergy and ministers, lay representatives from the local congregations, the participating denominations and the intermediate body should take place. When in any particular circumstances the appointing denomination cannot arrange this consultation, that denomination should advise the other partners on these circumstances.

☆ **Before the search** is undertaken for any new or additional minister, the responsible person in the appointing church is asked to notify the other churches involved and the intermediate body. It would be wise also to check that the other members of the LEP team have been told of the impending search.

☆ Candidates being asked to consider the vacancy should be supplied with a **circuit/parish/pastorate** profile which gives a brief description of the local ecumenical situation with information on the partnership or covenant. Copies of current key documents, such as the covenant and constitution, should also be provided.

☆ Any candidate likely to be appointed should **meet all the appropriate people** in the Local Ecumenical Partnership before the appointment is decided. This should include the existing clergy and ministers, lay representatives of the churches in the Local Ecumenical Partnership and a representative of the intermediate body. In their advisory capacity, these people should have the opportunity of expressing their opinion to those responsible for the appointment before the appointment is made. Where the Roman Catholic Church is the appointing denomination, the post may be filled quickly, but it is important that there is time for agreed ecumenical processes of consultation to be put into effect.

☆ As soon as possible after a decision has been made, the senior person involved in the appointing denomination locally should ensure that those who have taken part in this process are **informed of the decision.**

ii. Welcoming the new minister

The newly appointed minister should be welcomed into the LEP at an appropriate ecumenical service of induction, institution, commissioning or welcome. It is important that this service both meets the normal (and sometimes legal) requirements for initiating a new ministry in the appointing denomination, and makes a public statement about the commitment of the denominations to one another in the local situation. The participating denominations should all be represented at the service by a church leader or equivalent person, and where there is an ecumenical team its members should be given an opportunity to welcome the new minister as a colleague and renew their commitment to one another in the partnership.

It may be appropriate for the declaration of intent for the Local Ecumenical Partnership to be accepted by the appointed candidate in a clear expression of personal commitment to ecumenical working during the service.

A sample liturgy for Methodist/United Reformed Church joint churches is given in *Partners in Sharing and Commitment* (see bibliography).

iii. Preparation and training for ministry in an LEP

Once the new minister has been appointed to the LEP the county and denominational ecumenical officers should arrange to meet the new minister to discuss the local situation more fully. The County Ecumenical Officer should also arrange for the new minister to undergo appropriate training for ministry in an LEP. Training courses are run by Churches Together in England for staff recently appointed to LEPs, and information on these courses is available from county ecumenical officers and from the Field Officers of CTE (*see Appendix 8*). In Wales courses are available for those new to ministry, including those coming to work in LEPs. A range of other opportunities for gaining experience of a variety of local ecumenical contexts is also available, including guided visits to a number of ecumenical partnerships in Milton Keynes. Information on these and other opportunities is also available from county ecumenical officers.

Working in teams

Working in teams enables the insights not only of different individuals to be shared, but of the different traditions represented by those individuals. Working in teams also provides a model for ecumenical working where both issues and responsibility are shared. Sharing is a reflection of what the call to be ecumenical is about: not one tradition alone making decisions or taking responsibility on behalf of others, but different traditions coming together to share insights so that the church may be built up.

i. What is a team?

Teams can take many forms. They are at their best when well balanced but this is not always easy to achieve. They can comprise both men and

38

women, ordained and lay, or ordained only. Much of this chapter will look at the questions that arise in teams of ordained staff.

Teams occur in many places in each of the Christian traditions. In the Methodist Church for example, ministers in any one circuit work together as a team. In the Church of England, the word "team" has a technical use. In such a team, the words "rector" and "vicar" are used in a special sense, different from their traditional meanings. The incumbent is always styled "rector" and the other members of the team are styled "vicars". The setting up of Anglican teams relates to the effective deployment of ministry across an area (see *Pastoral Measure 1983* for further details). When a group of people work together within one tradition, ways of working and lines of authority are often clearer than in a group of people working together across traditions. For example, in the case of a rector and two vicars, it is clear where authority lies. Again, in a Methodist circuit with a team of Methodist ministers, one of them will have a clearly defined role as super-intendent, with specific responsibilities assigned to him or her for the circuit as a whole.

Many one-denominational teams also include lay people in a variety of ways. While in any one-denominational team, some areas of team life are simpler because of the shared tradition of understanding within that denomination, there are also, as in every team, areas that need working on. There can be different theological viewpoints, or difficulties in inter-personal relationships.

Working in an ecumenical team can involve similar challenges to those facing a one-denominational team – difficulties which can seem to out-weigh the advantage of the ecumenical nature of the team. On the other hand, it is also possible to have a greater richness and diversity in an ecu-menical team.

One-minister LEPs: an LEP in which there is only one minister can present a challenge as the task of fairly representing the different traditions in the LEP falls on the single full-time member of staff. Such ministers can also lack the support which a team can give. Careful attention needs to be given to developing good support networks, both with members of the con-gregations and with ministers of the same or other traditions from outside the LEP.

Two team LEPs: pressure is put on people when they serve simultane-ously in both a denominational team and an ecumenical team, for instance when there is an Anglican team ministry and an ecumenical team within the same LEP, or when a Methodist minister is in an ecumenical team and also part of the circuit staff team. This can lead to conflict in terms of team loyalty and of which team takes priority. It can also lead to a proliferation of team and staff meetings which can be seen as cutting against the underlying work of ministry. The question of working in two teams is one that needs to be carefully addressed when it occurs. Sometimes it is possible to free people from the denominational team in order that they may serve more fully in the ecumenical team.

ii. Identifying aims and objectives

A team needs to take time to identify its aims and objectives and to agree on these. There are varying views of what the church, a Christian, a minister, actually is in our different traditions. If underlying assumptions are not addressed, disagreements can arise which are unhelpful to the overall life and work of the LEP. The task of setting aims and objectives can in itself be a helpful one, particularly if these aims and objectives concentrate on what is achievable in any one area. It is probably more helpful to have as an aim "to plan a series of studies on the background of the Christian traditions in the LEP" or "to engage in a visitation to the neighbourhood" than a more general aim, such as "to bring in God's kingdom". The working out of the aims and objectives for the team can be a helpful way of understanding the aims and objectives of the LEP as a whole and the way the team fits in to it.

iii. Sharing Worship in a Team

The possibilities of shared work can also vary according to the denominations involved. For example, in a Free Church/Anglican team where there is a formal LEP agreement, either minister can celebrate the Eucharist. This offering of eucharistic hospitality is made possible by certain national agreements which have taken place in recent years (see *Appendix 4 for reference to B44 of the Church of England*). When it comes to an LEP with Roman Catholic involvement, this same arrangement is not possible. However, there are other forms of sharing that are possible, such as for an Anglican or Free Church minister to preach at a Roman Catholic service or for a Roman Catholic priest or sister to preach at an Anglican or Free Church service. These arrangements need to be agreed beforehand with the appropriate authorities.

iv. Understanding Different Models of Leadership

In a one-denominational team, there is usually a clearer understanding of where authority lies in that denomination. Work needs to be done in an ecumenical team in order to understand one another's denominational backgrounds, in particular each member's understanding of authority. It is easy to make denominational assumptions about leadership which are

40

inappropriate for an ecumenical team. A discussion about decision-making and leadership should take place at an early stage in the life of a team before too many things that need deciding actually occur.

It is important to develop a good process of appointing a team leader, to decide on the length of term of office of this person, and whether the leadership will pass from one member of the team to another at agreed intervals. A variety of models is possible. Each member of the team could be leader for one year, or the role of team leader could be assigned to a member who has particular responsibilities within the team. Whichever model is adopted, the role and responsibilities of the team leader should be mutually agreed.

v. Improving teamwork

The development of the life of any team takes a certain amount of work in itself. This is facilitated by having regular, weekly team meetings; by gathering together regularly to pray; and by participating in away days and retreats. Having a team consultant who will advise on such areas as relationships within the team and the sharing of work can also be a help. A local advisory group can sometimes help in discussions about team responsibilities and relationships.

Teams work on many different levels and help may be required with the emotional, rational, spiritual and organisational aspects of team life. Who should set the agendas for team meetings? Are minutes to be taken? Who is responsible for implementing any decisions made? Space must be made for what can be the very differing needs of each team member. It is also important to be clear about who is responsible for what in any one team, particularly when there are overlapping areas of responsibility such as the pastoral care of a congregation, student population or staff.

vi. Freeing people for particular tasks

There can be difficulties in ecumenical teams when people come together with different understandings of the church, personalities, skills and amount of time available. However, there can also be a great sense of being freed for particular tasks and of being able to share in companionship with people who are on the same ecumenical journey. Working ecumenically can enable a greater specialisation than is possible in ordinary parish work. One person can take on responsibility for youth work across the denominations, another for baptism, another for confirmation preparation. It is also then possible to free time for the mission tasks of the church. When fewer people are available in any one parish or congregation, the maintenance of the church can assume a higher priority; the time and energy of any one ministerial team member can be absorbed by such things as the new roof. In a larger ecumenical team, it is possible to delegate such areas of responsibility within the team and free more time for the church to play its proper role in reaching out to the wider community. However, if a larger team also has several church buildings in its care, further work needs to be done to free any one team member for a particular task.

vii. Changes in personnel

Change in team personnel is a matter that needs to be addressed very carefully. The arrival of a new member in the team does take a time of adjustment, both for the new member and for the existing team. The same process of adjustment needs to be gone through each time a new team member arrives; the already existing team is changed and due account needs to be taken of this by those already in place. The new team member should also be aware of the already established ways of working and understanding.

viii. Role of lay people

For the development of a wider ministry in an LEP, the involvement of lay people is important. Different traditions are used to involving lay people in different ways. An LEP can provide new and innovative ways for developing a real sense of partnership between lay and ordained.

If lay people are to be fully involved as part of a wider ministry team, careful attention needs to be given to the timing of meetings. Fixing meetings during usual working hours is not conducive to furthering the involvement of lay people. LEPs work best when the ministry of the whole people of God is harnessed together in witness and in service to the community.

There is a particular challenge to the churches in the later part of the 20th century that comes from the diminishing number of ordained people in many Christian traditions. This gives the task of taking the laity seriously a new imperative. This is not only a matter of involving lay people more fully in the internal life of the church, it is also about equipping members of congregations more fully for their Christian life in the world.

LEPs open up the possibility of developing collaborative, participative models of working in the church. Participation is enhanced by the spiritual contributions which people from different Christian traditions bring to bear. The involvement of the whole people of God in discussions about the way our traditions have varied across the centuries can lead to new and enriching understandings of faith.

Local Church Decision-Making

Different Christian traditions have varying understanding and practices when it comes to local church decision-making. For instance for the Church of England, the vicar and church wardens have particular responsibilities, as does the Parochial Church Council, whilst for Baptists, authority lies in the Church Meeting, which elects deacons to serve as a leadership body to oversee various areas of the church's life, on its behalf (for further details, see *A Harmony of Church Administration*, CTE 1995).

Some of the denominations nationally authorise the Ecumenical Council of an LEP to act as the decision making body in their tradition. For the United Reformed Church the Ecumenical Council is seen as the equivalent of Elders, for the Methodist Church it is seen as the equivalent of the Church Council, and for the Church of England, whilst certain matters may be delegated to the Ecumenical Council, many important decisions are required by statute to be taken by the Parochial Church Council. This can be achieved by the Annual Parochial Church Meeting (formally constituted within the annual meeting of the LEP) reconstituting the PCC each year in such a way that, in simultaneous and united session with the Ecumenical Church Council, any required Church of England business can be conducted by the PCC and minuted as such. Care needs to be taken to understand the differing role of these bodies in each of the different traditions and to develop the role of the Ecumenical Council so that it fulfils the obligations of the local decision-making bodies in each of the traditions.

The role of the regular Church Meeting, at which each member of the congregation is entitled to both speak and vote, is an interesting one in an LEP. It can be used as a forum for discussing key issues and can open up new possibilities for participating in decision making. However, the lines of authority of all the participating denominations have to be borne in mind in seeing what decisions are appropriate for a Church Meeting to take and what decisions need also to be referred to the wider councils of the church and those exercising episcopal authority.

Decision making can be a long and protracted process; but significant ecumenical growth is possible as people learn to be more tolerant of one another and more appreciative of each other's ways of making decisions. Although decision making can seem at times painfully slow, it can also offer useful models for conflict resolution. (*See also Chapter 6 for further discussion on aspects of authority.*)

Property in Local Ecumenical Partnerships

Detailed information on the provisions and application of the Sharing of Church Buildings Act 1969 can be found in: *"Under the Same Roof: Guidelines to the Sharing of Church Buildings Act 1969"* (CTE 1994).

The Sharing of Church Buildings Act 1969 provides an agreed legal framework for ecumenical living at the local level, expressed in a sharing agreement. The Act is a piece of enabling legislation, providing a means for churches to share buildings, to share and transfer funding, and give security of tenure to congregations moving in with one another. The Act also enables the shared construction of new buildings and allows marriage services according to the rites and ceremonies of the appropriate denominations. The Act permits in a shared building whatever would normally be allowed in a building belonging to participating denominations. It therefore enables a sharing of ministry and congregational life.

Sharing agreements can take time to prepare, although 25 years of experience since the Act was passed has established forms and precedents so that the process should now be easier. Sharing agreements should be fairly standard documents, and do not have to reflect the local variety of situations to the same extent as constitutions. Extensive consultation on sharing agreements can lead to excessive legal fees.

The Sharing of Church Buildings Act was originally envisaged as covering situations in which congregations using the same building wished to retain their own separate denominational identity. However, almost from the beginning it was used for new buildings, jointly owned by two or more denominations, with one united congregation, and there are relatively few situations remaining where congregations sharing the same building lead separate lives. In circumstances in which one congregation is a 'lodger' in a building owned by another this has often led to developing co-operation, even if they are unable fully to share their main worship service on a regular basis, as where one of the participating churches is Roman Catholic.

Some problems have arisen between Christian communities in large towns and cities with multi-ethnic populations, where informal arrangements for sharing church premises are made without the benefit of a sharing agreement, or a commitment to developing partnership by the congregations involved. Problems might arise when, for example, an independent Black-majority congregation rents space and time in a building owned by one of the mainstream denominations. Often the initial approach is handled by the church hall booking secretary on the same basis as a request from the badminton club. A landlord and tenant relationship is established and resentment and misunderstanding can develop, leading to the 'tenant' church, which may be a member of the national ecumenical structures, feeling hurt and rejected. *"The Sharing and Sale of Church Buildings"* (CTE 1994) provides useful guidelines on this.

The Sharing of Church Buildings Act does not automatically apply to all Christian churches, but those not named under the Act can be parties to sharing agreements if they apply to be "gazetted" under the terms of the Act. Further information on this process is available through County Ecumenical Officers and from the Co-ordinating Secretary for Church Life at CCBI (*see Appendix 8*).

In England the Group for Local Unity, a co-ordinating group of Churches Together in England, has particular responsibility for advising on sharing agreements; the secretary can be contacted care of CTE. In Wales advice and information can be obtained from the Ecumenical Commission of CYTUN (*see Appendix 8*).

5. SUPPORT, OVERSIGHT AND REVIEW

Intermediate bodies in England and Wales have responsibility as sponsoring bodies of LEPs, to provide support and oversight, evaluation and review. This chapter outlines the role of the intermediate bodies in both countries and looks in detail at how they carry out key tasks in connection with LEPs.

The role of intermediate bodies in England

In England there are now fifty intermediate bodies, many of which cover regions which are co-terminus with counties or metropolitan areas. The form and structure of the intermediate bodies varies from place to place, and they may be referred to by a variety of names – Sponsoring Body, Ecumenical Council, Churches Together in …, Church Leaders Meeting – which often reflect their origins and local development. That the intermediate bodies work in differing ways reflects the needs of their local contexts, and also the level of financial and other resources available; but the importance of all the intermediate bodies lies in their role as the 'filling' in the English ecumenical sandwich.

As with the other ecumenical instruments the source of authority for intermediate bodies lies in the commitment of the participating denominations to each other. For some denominations the imperative to participate in ecumenical relationships at the intermediate level comes from the commitment of their church to the ecumenical process at the national level; for other churches the imperative lies in the fact that individual congregations are committed to ecumenical working in local situations. Because of these differences in polity, the representatives of the denominations come to the intermediate body from churches with differing concepts of authority and structures for decision making, so not all have the same authority to speak and act on behalf of the denomination they represent.

The intermediate bodies enable contact and communication between those involved in local ecumenism and those working at the national level through Churches Together in England, give support to local ecumenism in all its forms, and encourage working together at the intermediate level on a wide range of concerns.

i. The intermediate body as the sponsoring body

In most instances the intermediate body acts as the sponsoring body for Local Ecumenical Partnerships and is responsible for enabling their establishment, supporting their life and overseeing a regular process of review or evaluation.

In this connection intermediate bodies:

☆ facilitate relationships between LEPs and their parent denominations;

☆ ensure that fair agreement is reached on the financial commitment of the denominations to the LEP and the LEP to the denominations;

☆ ensure that the project is neither swamped by the expectations of the parent denominations nor ignored by them;

☆ maintain relationships with LEPs through support groups, local advisory groups, consultants or other appropriate structures;

☆ bring the contribution and insights of the LEP to the wider church, and enable the LEP to feel part of that church;

☆ oversee policy decisions with respect to LEPs;

☆ ensure good practice in framing constitutions, making appointments and resourcing staff;

☆ set procedures for when staff are withdrawn or replaced;

☆ advise on worship and liturgy, and authorise forms of service;

☆ offer guidance in matters of discipline and law;

☆ resource the theological reflection of LEPs, especially in faith and order matters.

ii. Representation on intermediate bodies

The composition of the intermediate bodies is varied, some having only the church leaders, ecumenical officers and other denominational representatives while others include representatives from those involved in local ecumenism. The frequency of meetings varies from once a year to six times a year, and their funding and resources also differ widely.

iii. County Ecumenical Officers

Most intermediate bodies are serviced by an officer or secretary who is appointed jointly by the churches. This "County Ecumenical Officer" works across the area covered by the intermediate body to support and foster local ecumenical development of all kinds. Some county ecumenical officers or secretaries are full-time, some part-time and some "spare-time". In some places they also work on behalf of one or more of the partner churches as their denomination's ecumenical officer.

iv. Other work of the intermediate body

Intermediate bodies co-ordinate the denominations in working together at the county or metropolitan area level: this might focus on initiating work in specific areas such as local broadcasting or industrial chaplaincy, or it might be aimed at encouraging commitment and integration in working together for mission, education, social responsibility or youth work. The intermediate body works to put the ecumenical question *"could we be doing this together?"* on the agenda in every area of the church's life, and encourages sharing between the denominations in planning for the future and for the deployment of ministerial and other resources.

The intermediate body is also responsible for the support and encouragement of other kinds of local ecumenical development, in Councils of Churches, Churches Together and local ecumenical groups. It represents the churches in negotiations with local authorities and development corporations over ecumenical projects, and oversees the continuing relationship between the churches and these bodies.

v. Other ways of working together

The denominations have developed various models for working together at the intermediate level which reflect the view that the Churches Together structures should not establish a cumbersome additional layer of ecumenical activity, but are there to enable committed relationships and the sharing of resources between the denominations:

☆ **Joint work:** two or more denominations share resources in a particular task or appointment; for example, denominational staff involved in local broadcasting or industrial mission do work on that issue for the participating churches within the area covered by the intermediate body.

☆ **Co-ordinated work:** the churches share information about present working and future planning to avoid duplication of effort and expenditure.

☆ **Representative work:** one denomination works on behalf of all the partner churches as the lead agency in a particular area of work such as social responsibility

The intermediate level in Wales

In Wales the situation is different. Whereas in England it is normative for each county or metropolitan area to have some kind of intermediate body, in Wales the emerging pattern is of a few regional bodies (each covering more than one unitary authority). The principal aim of these regional bodies is to sponsor the existing LEPs in their area, and to identify potential LEPs. By the mid 1990s more than 60 LEPs had been registered in the whole of Wales, involving covenanted and non-covenanted churches in various combinations. Further information on LEPs in Wales, including a current copy of the 'List of Inter-Church Initiatives in Wales' can be had either from the General Secretary of ENFYS or CYTUN (*see Appendix 8 for addresses*).

Free Church partnerships are also a significant part of the Welsh scene. A Welsh language Consultative Committee on Ministry exists at the national level, under the auspices of the Free Church Council of Wales, in order to provide advice and support. It has its own network of regional committees. A particular feature of many of these arrangements is the concept of community ministries, where, in a given locality, a minister from one of the Free Church traditions will be recognised and funded to serve them all. Copies of 'Guidelines for Community Ministry' are available from denominational headquarters.

Further information on working at the intermediate level in England and Wales may be found in the handbook: "This Growing Unity", CTE 1995 (see bibliography).

Support and oversight for Local Ecumenical Partnerships

The support of Local Ecumenical Partnerships is the responsibility of the intermediate body, which acts on behalf of the participating denominations as the sponsoring body. In offering support for local ecumenism, the intermediate body works to enable the developing life of LEPs in both theological and practical ways, helping them to reflect on their experience of ecumenical living and providing suitable resource people to encourage the further development of the partnership. The support structure also exists to ensure that the development of the LEP remains within the bounds agreed by the parent denominations, and may act as an arbitrator in situations where conflict arises between the LEP and the parent denominations, or within the partnership.

The parent denominations delegate the responsibility for the support of LEPs to the intermediate body partly to avoid overburdening the LEP with multiple layers of relationship with ecumenical and denominational structures. However LEPs need to be in active and continuing relationship with the parent denominations, for example through representation on appropriate denominational bodies, so that they retain a sense of being part of the wider church and so that the wider church is able to benefit from their experience. The task of initiating and continuing relationships should not be the responsibility of the LEP, but of the participating denominations and the intermediate body.

The support structures also exist to help LEPs to raise potentially difficult issues with the denominational and ecumenical structures, and to enable a proper consultation in decision making processes about the future of a partnership. In some areas each LEP sends an annual report to the intermediate body, and the support structures may help with the formulation of this report.

Models for Support and Oversight

The intermediate body may exercise support and oversight for LEPs in a variety of ways.

i. Support Groups or Local Advisory Groups

The establishment of a support group for each LEP has the advantage of providing continuity in relating to the project and maintaining a good level of communications with the ecumenical and denominational structures. Relationships of trust and understanding can be built up through support groups, facilitating the process of consultation and follow-up when the partnership is reviewed or when staff are appointed. The disadvantages of this model for support are that, if the intermediate body is responsible for many LEPs, it can be a problem to find suitable people to serve in such groups; the support group may also feel like a burden to the LEP, as yet another group of people that the project has to relate to. It is sometimes helpful to appoint a support group for a particular period in the life of an LEP, for example when it is just beginning, or when undergoing a change in its life, or when it is undertaking a major building project or accepting another denomination into membership.

ii. Visits

In some areas support for LEPs is provided through formal visits by the County Ecumenical Officer and a small group of representatives from the sponsoring body. These visits may take place annually, and provide an opportunity to maintain communications, although perhaps not on a profound level. This may be a more sustainable model of support where an intermediate body is stretched to provide support for a large number of partnerships, and can be used to alert the intermediate body to the need for the provision of a support group if the partnership is undergoing difficulties or in a period of transition. Sometimes the responsibility for visiting LEPs and providing support for them is left entirely to the County Ecumenical Officer; this is not a satisfactory model for support, particularly since many ecumenical officers work part-time.

iii. Consultants

The intermediate body may choose to appoint one or more consultants to support the developing life of each LEP; the consultants maintain frequent contact with the partnership and report to the intermediate body at regular intervals.

iv. Twinning

The intermediate body may enable mutual support and encouragement between LEPs by establishing twinning relationships between partnerships in similar situations. This approach is sometimes used in asking two LEPs to review one another's partnerships, and has the advantage of enabling the cross-fertilisation of ideas between partnerships.

v. Support and Review

Support structures can play an important part in helping the review of an LEP to be an effective and positive process, through helping the LEP to prepare for the review and to reflect on the experience and the implementation of the recommendations. To avoid burdening the LEP with a complex and energy-consuming network of relationships it is good practice if denominational and ecumenical support and review can be linked.

Evaluation and Review

It is the responsibility of the intermediate body, in its capacity as the sponsoring body, to establish and resource a process of evaluation and review for Local Ecumenical Partnerships. Such reviews normally take place every five to seven years, as laid down in the constitution of the LEP.

As the ultimate purpose of a review is the extension of God's Kingdom, it is important that everyone involved approaches the review process prayerfully. Members, ministers and reviewers need to be clear about the positive aim and purpose of the review, and all those involved locally must be encouraged to participate in the process.

The review process is dependent on openness and a genuine wish to listen to what the reviewers have to say, and to develop the life of the partnership. This openness can be fostered by thorough preparation, with preliminary visits to share ideas and information about the review process with the LEP, so that everyone knows what to expect. Those involved locally should have the chance to question and shape the review process, so that it is suitable for their context. Practical issues are also important, such as ensuring that the venues for review meetings are suitable, and that appropriate hospitality can be provided for the reviewers.

How the review process is carried out will vary between intermediate bodies:

☆ There may be self evaluation, with the County Ecumenical Officer, LEP consultant or support group working with those involved locally to review the work of the partnership, and reflect on future possibilities for its development.

☆ The sponsoring body may appoint a review team of around three people, who will meet with members and ministers of the churches joining them for worship and for some other activities. They will try to get to know those involved, and to build up a picture of local church life. The review team will want to meet individuals and small groups, as well as attending events; they may also want to meet people in the community beyond the church, so that they can build up a picture of the LEP in its local context.

☆ A review may be conducted over an extended weekend, or over a period of several weeks or several months according to the needs of the area and the availability of the reviewers.

☆ The review process may be undertaken in co-operation between the intermediate body and one or more of the sponsoring denominations, and may be accepted as a review in denominational as well as ecumenical terms.

The local context gives to every partnership a distinctive flavour, and that context is formed by many things – geography, demography, history – quite apart from the issues around inter-church relationships. Because of this variety of local factors, it is difficult to set a blueprint for reviews, and the intermediate body may wish to ask that the review examine a particular area in the life of a partnership. However, it is always the task of

53

a review to listen to what is said, and what is unsaid; to understand the LEP in its context and to reflect with people in the LEP on future vision and development.

The review should examine the following areas:

☆ What is the story of the LEP?

☆ What is the context of the LEP?

☆ Have the supporting documents (constitution etc), helped the life of the partnership, and do they need re-writing to reflect recent development?

☆ What has been positive in the life of the partnership?

☆ What has been negative in the life of the partnership?

☆ What difference has the partnership made to inter-church relationships?

☆ What difference has the partnership made to the engagement of the churches with the life of the local community?

☆ Where have points for conflict or growth arisen?

☆ How do the structures of power operate within the LEP?

☆ Is the liturgical and spiritual life of the LEP sustaining and supporting the lives of its members in their ministry?

☆ What provision is there for learning together?

☆ What are relationships like between church leaders or clergy?

☆ Have appointments been made with appropriate ecumenical consultation?

☆ What is the financial position of the LEP?

☆ What about relationships with other churches in the area, and with the structures of the sponsoring denominations?

☆ What vision or dreams do the churches have for their future together?

Not all these questions will be relevant to all LEPs, and some LEPs will want to reflect on other areas. It is important that reviewers are flexible in their approach, so that they are able to listen, understand and reflect the LEP in its context. The review should look for growth both within the LEP and beyond it; growth both in extent and depth.

54

At the end of the process a review report will be compiled which might include some points of encouragement and recommendations for the LEP, for the intermediate body or for the sponsoring denominations. The County Ecumenical Officer, support group or consultant will meet with those involved to reflect on the reception and implementation of any recommendations.

(See also Revised Guidelines for the Review of LEPs, CTE December 1993)

6. CUTTING EDGES OF ECUMENICAL WORK

This handbook has looked at some of the practical issues to do with developing local ecumenical ways of working. While the main aim of the handbook is to help those who are specifically dealing with questions of local ecumenism, it has also endeavoured to place these questions within their national context and within some of the broader questions that working ecumenically raises.

Questions of principle as well as of practice arise: questions about the traditions' differing theological understandings, and of the holding together of a vision of unity that embraces not only our existing Christian traditions but the whole of God's created earth. The wider aspects of ecumenical working begin to touch on such areas as interfaith dialogue and the church's care for and relation to the whole of creation.

This final chapter focuses on the more particular inter-denominational questions that are raised when people of different Christian traditions come together. The chapter ends with a reflection on the wider goal of the unity towards which we work, and of the role of LEPs in relation to this wider goal.

Ecclesiology

This word relates to our understanding of the nature of the church. It is helpful in LEPs for ecclesiological questions to be addressed. What is the understanding of the nature of the church that we each bring from our own traditions? As each tradition looks to its own self-understanding and to the roots of that self-understanding, so a richer sense of the nature of the church across our different traditions can be experienced. As together we look at our roots in scripture and tradition, in reason and experience, so we rediscover for ourselves the purpose and calling of God in the life of the church. In the different Christian traditions, scripture, tradition, reason and experience have played different roles. When we come together, it is important to look again at those areas which have particularly shaped us so that we may engage in the ecumenical dialogue one with another.

Working locally on a renewed understanding of the nature of the church is also helpful when it comes to questions that deal with the relationship between the church and the world, and between Christianity and other faiths. These are areas of discussion that find a practical focus in an LEP as it seeks to engage in ministry and mission in the community in which it is set. It is good for this practical focus to be undergirded by a shared understanding of the nature of the church in order to be clear about the kind of mission that can be taken in any one local community and the kind of dialogue that can be engaged in with people of other faiths. For example, does it see its primary task as engaging in mission to a particular local geographical community, or as gathering a like-minded congregation of worshippers?

The area of ecclesiology embraces many particular aspects of the life of the church. Sometimes, one or another aspect will have a specific focus at any one time in the life of an LEP. The following paragraphs outline some aspects of ecclesiological questions, as they come to the fore in LEPs.

Lay Presidency

The role of lay people in the life of the church is understood differently in our different Christian traditions. For instance in some traditions lay people are fully involved at every level in the decision making processes of the church whilst in other traditions decision making is seen as the particular role of the ordained.

One of the many ways in which these differences can focus in an LEP is that of lay presidency at Holy Communion. In the Baptist tradition, it is understood that a person duly appointed by the Church Meeting may preside at Holy Communion. In the United Reformed Church the District Council can, in the case of a pastoral necessity, authorise lay presidency at Holy Communion by an elder and the Methodist Church very occasionally authorises a particular lay person for the same reason. However, this practice is not permitted in Anglican and Roman Catholic churches.

The issue of lay presidency at Holy Communion and the way it is resolved in an LEP illustrates one of the cutting edges of ecumenical working. Here is a matter which is accepted as a 'norm' in some traditions and yet is unheard of in other traditions. When people of these differing traditions come together there is a question about developing a policy which acknowledges both their practices and theologies.

One possible solution is that, if lay presidency is authorised to occur within an LEP, it is made clear that the service being held is of that one particular tradition rather than an ecumenical service approved by the whole LEP. Only lay people of the traditions that authorise lay people to do so may preside at Holy Communion and only in the way that is duly authorised by those traditions.

Authority and Decision-Making

Each of the major Christian traditions has a different approach to authority and decision making. It is important for the LEP to find out what is required by the participating denominations before making decisions. It may be necessary to have meetings to decide who decides!

In some traditions, authority is focused in the Church Meeting (for instance, of the local congregation in the Baptist Church). In some it is focused in a council of the church (such as the Methodist Church Council or URC District Council); in some, in the priest or the bishop (Roman Catholic Church). Authority is a complex matter in the Christian tradition. It is important to take careful account of the differing appreciations of where authority is to be found, and who is required to make decisions on which matters.

In an LEP decision-making can be a prolonged process as each denomination's method of operating comes into play. Decision-making may also vary with regard to the kind of issue involved. For example:

☆ If it is a matter of making a major alteration to a building, this needs to be referred to the relevant authorities in the Anglican and Catholic Dioceses, the URC District Council, the Methodist Circuit Meeting, and to the Church Meeting as far as Baptists are concerned, as well as any other decision-making bodies within the LEP itself, such as, in a shared building, the Joint Council.

☆ When it comes to matters of faith or doctrine, such as the question of baptism and the baptism of those previously baptised in infancy, or the question of inter-communion between different Christian traditions, authority can more often be seen to lie at a national or international level,with the various agreements that are arrived at in the appropriate councils of the churches.

The exploration of the processes of decision making can lead to a renewed understanding of the appropriate role of authority in the life of the church. Each tradition acknowledges that it looks to that authority which comes from the triune God. The grappling with questions to do with authority and decision making can lead to a renewed understanding of the ways in which authority is received from God.

Questions about Baptism

There are sensitive questions raised in our different traditions with regard to baptism. While for some of our traditions the baptism of infants is the norm, for other of our traditions baptism can only actually happen for believers. This can lead to a variety of views with regard to baptism. For some people infant baptism is not regarded as valid. For others, baptism of believers who have already been baptised in infancy is re-baptism, apparently denying the effectiveness of baptism in infancy.

While the World Council of Churches report called *"Baptism, Eucharist and Ministry"* (see bibliography) has brought about a considerable convergence in mutual recognition of baptism, there is still a significant difference between some traditions when it comes to the question of the baptism of those previously baptised in infancy. The question is raised in particular by churches which believe that baptism needs to follow a profession of faith by the one being baptised. The issue surfaces in LEPs when individuals come to faith as adults, having been baptised much earlier in life, and then feel they want to make a public affirmation of their faith which finds its natural focus in baptism by immersion. In LEPs where traditions with differing views on baptism are represented, the question of re-baptism can be quite sharply felt. It is important that LEPs which include both churches which baptise infants and those which baptise only on a personal profession of faith should have an agreement in advance on what to do should the need arise.

The Baptist Union of Great Britain and the Methodist Church have recently published guidelines for procedures to follow when this happens (*see Appendix 5*). This document outlines the possibility of baptism being administered a second time in an LEP, with the person who has then been so baptised being transferred onto the Baptist membership roll rather than being on the joint membership roll. The guidelines go some way towards alleviating the differences, but do not overcome the fundamental disagreement.

The 1994 LEPs consultation in Swanwick affirmed that "Baptism and Re-baptism" was a topic of particular sensitivity and an urgent subject for agreement.

It was subsequently agreed by the Enabling Group of Churches Together in England that a high-level group should be set up to look further at this issue, to take account of the bi-lateral agreements and discussion between churches on this issue.

Confirmation and Church Membership

The different traditions have distinct views about what belonging to the church means and about what the outward and visible sign of this should be. Once more, in an LEP account needs to be taken of the views of the different traditions involved.

The 1994 LEPs Consultation at Swanwick, in its discussion on church membership, helpfully asserted the following:

"We affirm that as people are called to follow Christ they are incorporated into the life of the church in a variety of ways expressed through our different traditions.

Whatever the process we all recognise incorporation into the Church as being:
— in the context of a local congregation
— in a wider denomination
— part of the universal church of Christ.

Our traditions place the emphasis at different points, but all contain expressions of this three-fold reality.

Whether the emphasis is on the Grace of God or the commitment of the individual, most of our member churches recognise that such incorporation involves a baptismal initiation process expressing the faith of the church and of the individual.

Drawing on the report Christian Initiation and Church Membership *(BCC 1988) we value the concept of 'belonging' with an emphasis on participation within a Christian community. This has a particular importance for those local communities involving the Roman Catholic Church."*

i. Ecumenical Confirmation

Recent years have seen a growing development of joint services of confirmation by the Church of England and the Free Churches. In an LEP it is possible, in some traditions, for a person, having previously been baptised, to be jointly confirmed into the life of the participating denominations.

Joint confirmations need to take account of the practices of the traditions involved. In each case, the primary local minister has responsibility for presiding. However, who this is varies from tradition to tradition. For the Church of England, the bishop must take part in the act of confirmation. For the other traditions, it is the local ministers and also lay people from the congregation who take part, as people are welcomed into the life of that congregation. Different traditions can be involved in different ways according to the self-understanding of their own tradition. Thus, it is not necessary to have a URC Moderator and a Methodist Chairman of District present at confirmations. In the URC and the Methodist Church, the understanding of ministry is, at this point, slightly different from the Anglican understanding. The role of the URC Moderator and the Methodist Chairman of District does not include the practice of taking part in confirmations as they are not the primary local ministers. Those who confirm or receive into church membership in these two traditions are the local ministers. Therefore, it is possible to have local Free Church ministers taking part alongside the Anglican bishop and laying hands on each candidate at the same time. It is important to respect the different understandings of each tradition at this point.

Those involved in the confirmation service must be people who are properly authorised in their own traditions. It would be inappropriate for an Anglican priest who is "recognised and regarded" by the Methodist Church to participate in the same way at a service of confirmation as a Methodist minister.

While all the main Christian traditions allow for the possibility of the baptism of adults, there is a particular opportunity in an LEP with Baptist involvement to combine a service of believer's baptism and an ecumenical confirmation, if the candidate has not been previously baptised. At such services, those who have offered themselves are recognised as members of all the local participating churches whether Baptist, United Reformed, Methodist or Church of England, and are equally entitled to share in all the responsibilities and privileges of membership of the participating traditions.

There have been one or two instances in England where it has proved possible, with the agreement of the appropriate authorities, to hold a parallel confirmation between the Roman Catholic Church and other churches, but in this case joint membership of the churches is not given.

ii. Multiple and Extended Membership

Questions arise in LEPs about the difference between those who have been ecumenically confirmed into all the traditions that make up the LEP, and those who, before coming to this particular LEP, have been confirmed/received into church membership in only one tradition. There are times when the latter group of people feel deprived because they are not able to become full members of all the participating traditions. The 1994 Consultation on LEPs at Swanwick helpfully drew out this question as it arises in LEPs.

"Where there is shared ministry, congregational and worship life involving combinations of the Church of England and the Free Churches,

62

we believe there is now a new moment of opportunity to build on the sense of belonging. Many of those joining LEPs want to give expression to this by becoming members of more than one tradition. This has been recognised in many of them by what is described as Multiple Membership. This admission is into the full privileges and responsibilities of membership of the participating denominations. (If a member moved from an LEP to a church of a single denomination then they retain membership of that denomination to which they transfer.) However, those who, in many instances, founded the LEP and were already members of one tradition have been excluded from this wider joy. We believe this position, which causes unnecessary hurt and pain, should be rectified by enacting appropriate denominational legislation to permit what is often referred to as Extended Membership.

Multiple Membership

This occurs in those Local Ecumenical Partnerships where, through a joint Initiation or Confirmation Service, certain denominations can confer full initiation and communicant status on the same candidate simultaneously. (This generally means Anglican, Baptist, Methodist and United Reformed only but can involve others, though not Roman Catholics)

Extended Membership

Is about Multiple Membership being conferred without any further initiation rite on those communicant members of a Local Ecumenical Partnership whose denominations would permit it.

Recommendations

Within our definition of LEPs, which we understand to include so-called single church LEPs as well as LEPs involving two or more traditions we recommend:

1. *That there be opportunity for joint admission to membership/joint confirmation conveying on those so confirmed/admitted what is popularly described as multiple membership.*
2. *That the decision making bodies of the major Free Churches be invited to consult together with the Church of England with a view to the enacting of denominational legislation to permit LEPs to have so-called 'Extended Membership'."*

iii. Membership Returns

If there is a sharing agreement in place, there is a legal requirement to keep separate membership lists for each denomination. However, many LEPs will keep one list, with an added note on the list of each person's denomination. Each denomination has its own requirement with regard to membership returns. This is often the only moment within the life of an LEP at which members have to be identified by their denominations. It would be helpful to work towards some national agreement of the shape, content and timing of membership returns. Work has been done on this and it is hoped that progress will be made that will shorten the task of filling out denominational returns. There is a particular need to be clear about what happens when people are confirmed in two or more traditions, and the way these figures need to be shown in any annual return.

Ecumenical confirmation can confuse denominational statistics. Is it a matter of dividing them into percentages between each of the denominations involved in that LEP, or of returning them on a separate list to each denomination, clearly identifying that they are ecumenical confirmations and now belong to all the traditions who have participated in that service? Here is another opportunity to be at the forefront of the life of the church. Baptism and confirmation are given by God to the church as a means of incorporation into Christ and the church. Ecumenical confirmations highlight the faith that we share.

iv. When people move area

The question is sometimes raised of where people go to when they move away from an area in which they have been part of an LEP congregation, and go to a new area in which there is no similar LEP congregation. However this question also arises when people leave a one-denominational congregation. Denominational loyalty is not necessarily the only factor taken into account when looking for a church in a new area. Questions of the style and the shape of worship, the friendliness of a community, and the opportunities afforded by the weekday life of the church will shape people's decision. For many, there is a time of searching until they find a congregation in which they feel at home and able to play a part. People who move away from LEPs where they have had a good experience of ecumenical working are sometimes frustrated by not finding the same experience elsewhere. However, those who move away from LEPs to an area where there are none can provide a stimulus for the development of ecumenical work in that part of the country.

The Future of LEPs

Local ecumenical working has developed in a variety of ways. Some ecumenical partnerships have been made possible because of particular contexts, for example, new housing estates. The danger then is that local ecumenical working becomes identified with specific situations and is seen as being limited to them. However, the growth of village ecumenism and covenants in suburban areas illustrates that a variety of different models of working are possible.

Are LEPs possible in every area? LEPs are possible wherever people choose to make a commitment to join with people of other Christian traditions in worship, or prayer, or study, or mission, or community action. With the increasing variety of models of local ecumenical working that are available, people in different areas of the country can look at their own area and tradition to see what it is that God is calling them to do with one another in that place.

When there are clusters of LEPs working together, a further question arises about the way in which the denominational structures themselves can come closer together. If there is a large concentration of LEPs within a particular geographical area, they may find the pressure of relating to several different denominations all at once quite daunting. Is it then possible to develop new ways of structural working, at Methodist Circuit, Deanery Synod, URC District Council level?

The recent regional development of ecumenical structures is encouraging. But questions still remain about what powers the denominations are actually willing to hand over to regional structures to enable them to be more effective. The other side of this question is how regional structures should be constituted to be accountable to the denominations for the powers entrusted to them.

LEPs provide a challenge to those who say "it won't work" or "it can't be done". Much of the life in LEPs is about saying that it **can** work and it **can** be done, that it **will** work and it **will** be done. This insight from LEPs, that things are possible and do happen when Christians of different traditions come and share together, offers an insight to the main Christian traditions regionally and nationally. If it can be done locally, this gives a sign of hope for working towards national reconciliation between different traditions. The fact that it can be done locally provides a challenge to think again about what the Holy Spirit is moving the churches to become.

The future of LEPs lies in a continuing development of new models and in incorporating insights from other Christian traditions not so often found in LEPs, such as the Black-majority Churches, the Salvation Army, the Friends and the House Churches.

Working Towards Unity

The visible unity of all God's people is the larger backdrop to the work that goes on in local ecumenism. LEPs at their best are a foretaste of what might be when the main Christian traditions come together.

However, even in an LEP it is not always easy to capture that vision of belonging to the wider whole. The innovative work that is done ecumenically in LEPs at the forefront of the life of the church can lead to its own feeling of isolation from the denominations involved in the LEP. When this is added to people's natural parochialism, there are times when those involved in an LEP, especially if they are new Christians, cannot perceive the importance of being strongly related to the wider Christian denominations.

Are LEPs in danger of becoming a new church, with a life of their own that is not rooted within the life of the main Christian traditions? In fact the way in which diversity is experienced and held together in an LEP can be a sign of possibility for the main Christian traditions. The way in which the Holy Spirit can free us from inessentials to a new awareness of those things that lie at the heart of our faith can be a sign of hope for the ecumenical pilgrimage nationally.

The shape of visible unity and its acknowledgement of the rich diversity of all God's people is a major focus for discussion, both nationally and internationally (in England the "Called To Be One" process, and internationally, "Baptism, Eucharist and Ministry" and the 1993 Faith and Order Conference at Santiago, are some examples of the discussions taking place).

Whatever our vision of unity, there is a need for the experience of LEPs to be fed back into the denominations and for the experience of the denominations to be communicated to the LEPs. There is a sense in which the status of LEPs is always "provisional". They are on the frontiers of ecumenical ministry. They do not happen in one fixed pattern. They are not immune from the difficulties which can affect any one-denominational church, such as lack of resources, inter-personal conflicts, concentration on maintenance rather than mission; but they can form the ground for much experimentation and much rich development of the Christian life.

While LEPs, at their best, are a foretaste of the unity of all God's people, they provide hints of what is possible rather than a grand blueprint for a future united Church.

☆ At their best LEPs provide models of reconciliation for the wider community of the church and the world. In LEPs it is possible to look again at the way in which disputes are handled and resolved.

66

☆ The diversity of shared lifestyle demonstrates once more that Christianity is not a monochrome religion but embraces the wide variety of life reflected in God's gift of creation.

☆ LEPs can be a model for a renewed human community as they engage in the issues of the place in which they are set and embrace the people of that place.

☆ Learning not just tolerance of differences, but how to celebrate legitimate diversity can bring about an openness that causes people outside the church to feel welcomed and accepted.

☆ In LEPs it is possible to learn and experience again what it means to be inclusive, an inclusiveness based on the kind of inclusive love that God has for all his people.

Jesus prayed that all his people might be one. LEPs seek to live in the spirit and the power of that prayer, relying not on their own strength but on the strength of the God whose gift is unity.

APPENDICES

1. Denominational Statements

    Section 1 – The Baptist Union of Great Britain
    Section 2 – The Church of England
    Section 3 – The Methodist Church
    Section 4 – The Roman Catholic Church
    Section 5 – The United Reformed Church

    Note: these are not officially agreed statements, but represent the understanding of the individual author, in most cases the national ecumenical officer of the denomination concerned.

2. *Full text of Working Together in the new Ecumenical Instruments: Suggested Rules of Good Practice*, CTE 1991.

3. An example covenant

4. Text of Canons B43 and B44 of the Church of England (for details of complete explanatory booklet see bibliography)

    Note: Canons B43 and B44 are the copyright of the Central Board of Finance of the Church of England and are reproduced by permission.

5. Full text of the *Baptist/Methodist Agreement on Baptismal Policy*

6. *Elements of an effective LEP* from the report of the Consultation on the Future of LEPs held in March 1994.

7. Full text of *Model Constitutional Guidelines for a joint Methodist and United Reformed Church*

8. Useful addresses

APPENDIX 1

1: The Baptist Union of Great Britain
by Gethin Abraham-Williams, updated by Keith G. Jones

Decision Making

With its doctrine of the gathered community, the ultimate authority for a Baptist church, which is regulated by its Trust Deed and Rules, is the local Church Meeting. There has, therefore, to be reference back to the Church Meeting for all major decisions. This may take place monthly and all those on the Membership Roll are eligible to attend. It also appoints men and, in most cases, women to serve for a specific term as elders and/or deacons who, with the minister form a partnership. Elders, (if appointed) have a role in a team setting with the minister, to provide pastoral and spiritual oversight; the emphasis of the work of the diaconate being towards the good ordering of the life of the church, visiting etc.

Baptists believe in interdependency and are not pure independents as some imagine. Beyond the local church they work together in larger units of which the Association (which is the oldest) is usually county size, and the Union, national. Associations are grouped together in larger administrative areas, of which there are twelve. Each area has a General Superintendent who represents the Union and is available to offer advice and guidance. The Baptist Union meets as an assembly once a year, to which each member church may send its minister and other representatives. The life of the denomination in between times is regulated by the Baptist Union Council. The role of the General Secretary has greater importance than that of the annually elected President.

Churches choose to belong to the Association and to the Union, and some can be in one and not the other, though they usually join both. Neither the Association nor the Union has authority over the local church, but joining implies acceptance of responsibility to share in mutual fellowship, support and encouragement.

Some larger Associations and the Baptist Union are incorporated as

Trust Bodies for local churches and therefore have a significant role to play in the decisions made about sale and purchase of property, legal matters and adherence to the Trust Deed.

Ministry

It is the Church Meeting that calls a man or woman to be its minister, normally without time limit. It may also terminate a call! Unless it is Home Mission Fund aided, a Baptist church has to meet the full costs of its minister's salary, housing and working expenses. (Churches subscribe to the Home Mission Fund as they are able and inclined, but a per capita figure is recommended annually.)

There is a wide variety of dress amongst Baptist ministers, though some wear a gown, Geneva or academic (with or without hood), to conduct worship. A very few will don a cassock to take services. Some ministers also wear a clerical collar for everyday use.

Worship

Two Sunday services are normal, one in the morning geared to families, with most churches providing a Sunday school concurrently, and one in the evening often angled towards youth. Services consist of prayers, hymns, scripture readings and a sermon, by which great store is set, its anticipation and analysis entered into with relish! Where a church has a minister, he or she will usually conduct the worship at least three out of every four Sundays a month. Other churches rely on lay preachers. The degree to which a church has been affected by liturgical and charismatic renewal will often depend on its minister's interests.

Two important worship resources are: "Patterns and Prayers for Christian Worship" – a worship manual (Baptist Union Publications 1990) and "Baptist Praise and Worship" – a hymnbook with prayers, responses, psalms etc (OUP 1991)

Baptism and Church Membership

There is no particular age when a candidate is expected to be ready for Believers' Baptism, though most would probably be in their mid-teens. The criterion is an ability to make a declaration of a personal faith in, and commitment to, Jesus Christ. Baptismal services occur as the need arises after suitable preparation by the minister, or by other members appointed by the deacons.

They usually take place in a baptistry in the church, though swimming pools, rivers and the sea have sometimes been used! In a church baptistry, the water is normally warmed by portable immersion heaters to take off the chill! Prior to the baptism, the minister publicly questions each candidate: "Do you acknowledge Jesus Christ as your Saviour and Lord?" ("I do") "Do you promise with the help of the Holy Spirit to serve him in the church and in the world unto your life's end?" ("I do").

The minister then descends into the water and the candidates, now bare footed, follow one at a time. The women are dressed in simple baptismal gowns, with weighted hems and the men in white shirts and trousers. The minister may be dressed as the candidates are, or with waders under a preaching gown.

In the water, the minister will say to each candidate: "(Christian name), upon a profession of your faith and at your own request I baptise you in the name of the Father, the Son and the Holy Spirit." The candidate is then immersed, either from standing up or kneeling, until the water momentarily covers the head.

As each candidate is baptised, it is customary for the congregation to sing a verse of an appropriate hymn, or scripture song often chosen by the candidate.

The new Christians are received into membership with the right hand of fellowship and/or by the laying on of hands at communion, which either follows baptism or on a succeeding Sunday.

Many churches also allow membership on the basis of a public declaration without baptism, i.e. on 'profession of faith'. Every application for membership must be approved by the Church Meeting.

Communion

The majority of Baptist churches usually celebrate communion (sometimes referred to as The Lord's Supper) twice a month during or after a morning and evening service. A significant number celebrate less frequently or weekly. The deacons take it in turn to prepare the table with a common loaf on patens, though some churches still prepare small cubes of bread. Some use a single chalice for the wine, generally non-alcoholic, though many use the individual small cups. The table is covered with a white cloth.

Communion is normally conducted by the minister, though a senior deacon or visiting preacher, lay or ordained, may preside in his or her absence. At the communion table the deacons are seated on either side of the minister and assist in the administration, taking the elements to the people in their places. These are received and consumed in silence, or to the accompaniment of a suitable voluntary. Usually the bread is eaten as it is received and the cup retained so that all may drink it together. In common with other Free Church people, Baptists may well find it difficult to go forward to take communion and to receive from a common cup.

There is no set form of liturgy, but the pattern and wording of I Corinthians 11 is normally adhered to with the Prayer or Prayers of Thanksgiving offered by the minister or an elder or deacon.

It is usual in all but closed membership churches (i.e. open only to those baptised as believers) for an invitation to be given at the beginning of the service that 'our Table is open to all who love the Lord'. Such an invitation extends to all, whether or not any public profession of faith leading to membership (of any tradition) has been made.

After the service the unconsumed elements are disposed of in a variety of ways, but always in a reverent fashion.

Sensitivities

Baptists place great emphasis on freedom of conscience. This can create difficulties for other denominations when those baptised in infancy request Believers' Baptism! Baptists by and large, though, do not accept that the baptism of infants is a variant of the Baptism of Believers.

Many Baptist churches also accept as members those dedicated as infants who later make a 'profession of faith' and who have, therefore, missed out on any experience of baptism.

They regard evangelism as normative, encouraging and developing all forms of youth and missionary work.

Further information from Baptist Union of Great Britain, Baptist House, PO Box 44, 129 Broadway, Didcot, Oxon OX11 8RT. Telephone: 01235 512077.

2: The Church of England
by Donald Reece

Decision Making

The Church of England is organised into parishes, deaneries, forty four dioceses and the provinces of Canterbury and York. In the **parish**, policy is made by the Vicar (or Rector), churchwardens and the Parochial Church Council acting together. In some matters the approval of the Annual Parochial Church Meeting (all on the Electoral Roll) is required. This must meet before the end of April to adopt the reports and accounts of the year ending December 31st. The Church Representation Rules provide for baptised members of other trinitarian churches, without discarding existing membership, to belong to the Electoral Roll of their parish; stand for election to the PCC (with the permission of the bishop); and stand for election to the Deanery Synod.

The **deanery** is a grouping of between ten and twenty parishes presided over by the Rural (or Area) Dean, who is nominated by the bishop on the recommendation of the clergy. There is a lay co-chairman elected by lay members of the synod. The deanery synod has few executive powers, and functions primarily in advisory and co-ordinating capacities.

All the clergy of the deanery, together with the parochially elected lay representatives are the respective electors for members of the Houses of Laity and of Clergy in both the Diocesan and General Synods. The latter deals with major doctrinal and legislative matters. In some cases the approval of Parliament is also required. The bishop of the **diocese** with his Diocesan Synod and its committees (such as pastoral and finance) are the diocesan policy-making, financial and administrative executive. This includes the agreed parochial assessments (quota) being paid to the diocese.

The Archdeacon, as well as supporting the bishop in pastoral oversight and clergy appointments, has responsibility for the structure and furnishing of church buildings. This is governed by the Faculty Jurisdiction Rules which require advice from the Diocesan Advisory Committee and the issue of a faculty by the Diocesan Chancellor. The Archdeacon in his annual visitation of parishes is sometimes assisted by the Rural Deans. He also admits churchwardens as officers of the bishop, as well as of the parish.

Ministry

The ordained ministry of the bishop, the priests and deacons, whether paid or non-stipendiary, is fundamental to the life of the church and the diocese. Each parish has a priest as incumbent (Vicar or Rector). The current increase in lay ministries illustrates the emerging collaborative style involving both clergy and laity. Readers are unpaid, fully trained licensed lay ministers, while Church Army Sisters or Captains are amongst stipendiary lay ministers and community workers. Some dioceses create systems for training lay pastoral assistants, and some of these receive a certificate at the end of their course. A diocese will also provide part or full time lay or ordained ministry in such sectors as mission, unity, education, and social responsibility.

In rural areas it is usual for an incumbent to be responsible for more than one parish, in some cases as many as seven or eight. Also found, particularly in rural areas, are group and team ministries.

In a group ministry the clergy remain independent, but commit themselves voluntarily to mutual sharing of ministry. A team ministry, on the other hand, involves a legal commitment of the team Vicars and other licensed clergy and laity to one another, under the leadership of the team Rector. Specialist ministries may also be allocated amongst them. Within a team Ministry, PCCs may remain distinct, or one PCC may be established for the team, with district councils for the separate parishes.

Marriage in the parish church, after Banns and according to the rites of the Church of England, is the right of anyone resident in the parish, or on the Electoral Roll, if the usual conditions are fulfilled. A guide for parish clergy was issued in 1992, Anglican Marriages in England and Wales. Those who have been divorced and whose previous spouse is still alive, do not have this right, but local clergy may decide to exercise their right under civil law to conduct the marriages of such people, and in some dioceses guide lines for this are laid down by the bishop. However, it is still the exception rather than the rule for such marriages to take place in church. It must also be noted that the law enabling marriage in the Church of England is NOT interchangeable with the parallel legislation for marriage by other churches.

Much of the time of parish clergy is spent in the ministry of baptisms, marriages and funerals. Increasingly, lay people share in the pastoral aspects of this work. This illustrates the Church of England's sense of pastoral responsibility for everyone resident within the parish. Parish boundaries are statutory, and so a correct and courteous approach is required, either in ministry to residents of another parish, or if wider new ministry is being considered.

Worship

The incumbent and the PCC will decide how to effect the required provision (under Canon B3) of the Sunday services of Morning and Evening Prayer and Holy Communion, and any additional services. They may choose to use either the *Book of Common Prayer* (1662) or the *Alternative Service Book* (1980) for these services and for baptisms, weddings and funerals. Routine provisions for preaching, music, etc. are the responsibility of the Vicar.

The *Ecumenical Relations Measure* (1989) and related *Canons B43* (Of Relations with Other Churches) and *B44* (Of Local Ecumenical Projects) allow for a sharing of ministry with churches so designated by the Archbishops. This may include both lay or ordained ministers of other churches leading their worship in an Anglican Church, and also Anglican clergy participating in the worship of another church. The Diocesan

Ecumenical Officer will advise, and the *Ecumenical Relations Code of Practice 1989*, is an essential guide.

Weekday worship usually includes one or more celebrations of the Eucharist and there is a requirement for Morning and Evening Prayer to be said. House meetings for prayer and bible study are becoming more common, and sometimes are ecumenical.

Baptism and Confirmation

The baptism of adults and of infants are provided for. *The Book of Common Prayer* urges parents not to defer bringing their new born infants for baptism, and to see that they are brought to the bishop to be confirmed. The *Alternative Service Book* provides an integrated set of services which begins with that for baptism, confirmation and Holy Communion. Currently, a growing proportion of those seeking confirmation have not been baptised in infancy. Parishes vary in their preparation of and expectations for the professed faith of parents who seek baptism for their infants; but godparents must themselves have been baptised, and are expected to have been confirmed. An increasing number of parishes administer baptism at the main Sunday service of worship.

Admission to Holy Communion generally follows confirmation by the bishop. Very limited experimentation has been granted to some parishes to admit children to Holy Communion prior to their confirmation. Preparation for confirmation is commonly for about six months. Each diocese publishes guidelines for the minimum age of candidates for confirmation (usually 11 years), but many will be a few years older. The limited availability of the bishops to come to the parishes means that in each year congregations are grouped together for confirmations.

Where there is a Local Ecumenical Partnership, under Canon B44, the House of Bishops has made provision for a joint confirmation, at which each candidate receives the laying on of hands from the bishop and also from the confirming minister of other churches which are partners in the project. Such Christians will then locally exercise a dual or multiple church membership.

Holy Communion, Eucharist or Lord's Supper

Holy Communion, whether according to the Book of Common Prayer, Alternative Service Book or other authorised rite, must be presided over by a priest of the Church of England, or by one episcopally ordained in orders accepted by the Church of England. The distribution of the sacrament may be undertaken by deacons, readers or other lay people authorised within the diocese; or under the provisions of Canon B43, by appropriate members of other churches. Both the sacrament of Christ's Body and of Christ's Blood are administered to each person. Either wafers or bread may be used; the wine used should be alcoholic. There is one cup (chalice) for the wine, but for reasons of hygiene a few communicants may receive the wine by the intinction (dipping) of the bread. In some parishes consecrated bread and wine are reserved in an aumbry (a wall safe in the sanctuary) and later taken to the sick. Extended Communion would describe the extension of one celebration of Holy Communion by the taking of the consecrated elements by a deacon, reader or authorised lay minister to another congregation meeting on the same day in a separate church, usually within the same group or team. The Eucharist may also be celebrated in the homes of the housebound.

Parishes in a Local Ecumenical Partnership may, under Canon B44, have an agreement to share ministry, in which a minister of another church ordained for word and sacraments may preside at a Eucharist in a parish church using a customary rite of that church, or a rite authorised by the Church of England. Such a service, however, should not be held to be a celebration of the Holy Communion according to the use of the Church of England.

Canon B15A requires the admission to Holy Communion of baptised members who are communicants in good standing of other churches which subscribe to the doctrine of the Holy Trinity.

Sensitivities

It is helpful for members of other Churches to understand Anglican sacramental practices.

The baptism of an infant is effective, even if the faith of sponsors, and consequent Christian nurture is deficient. If someone baptised in infancy comes to personal faith as an adult, then the outward rite of baptism may not be repeated.

At Holy Communion, Canon B44 does not envisage anyone presiding other than one ordained to the ministry of Word and Sacraments. Also, when the people have received the sacraments, what is left over should be consumed, so that no consecrated bread or wine is returned to storage or thrown away.

Where there is ecumenical ministry, forethought is helpful, and guidelines on such matters may be worked out amongst the partner churches.

Further information from the Ecumenical Advisor for your diocese, or from the Local Unity Secretary, Council for Christian Unity, Church House, Great Smith Street, London SW1P 3NZ. Tel: 0171-222 9011.

Appendix 1

The process of appointment of a Vicar or Rector includes representation by members of the PCC and the right of presentation by the Patron (who may be an individual, a college or corporate body, a diocesan board or the bishop himself). It is the bishop when then institutes the priest to the parish. (See the Patronage (Benefices) Measure, 1986.)

3: The Methodist Church
by David Willie

1. Decision Making

The annual Conference meeting for ten days in June/July is the supreme authority. It consists of equal numbers of ministers and lay people, most of them elected by the District Synods. All ministers are ordained at services associated with the Conference and by its authority. The work of the church is serviced by units, representing various areas of work, responsible to the Conference. Methodists use the term "the Connexion" to refer to the Methodist Church in general and its national network.

The church in Great Britain is divided into 33 districts each with a chairman and each holding a twice-yearly Synod. They are a link between the Conference and the circuits. Every church is part of a circuit under the care of a Superintendent minister. The Superintendent is endowed with considerable authority and can do much to promote or to thwart the progress of an LEP. The Circuit Meeting elects representatives to the District Synod, invites ministers, and co-ordinates the work of local churches, each of which is represented on it.

The life of the local church, including the management of property, is ordered by a Church Council, which appoints a Pastoral Committee and other committees which may be required. In local ecumenical partnerships an ecumenical church council may serve as the church council with certain conditions. In ecumenical areas the meeting responsible for the general management of the area may act as the Circuit Meeting. The financial year ends on 31 August.

Ministry

All ministers are in the last resort under the direction of the Stationing Committee, which presents its recommendations for the 'stations' for the year beginning in September for approval by the Conference. Since all ministers move at that time there are no inter-regna in the circuits except in cases of emergency. A minister is appointed to the circuit and not to an individual church, and he or she can be redeployed within the circuit under the direction of the Superintendent and after consultation. In ecumenical areas the initial invitation is for seven years instead of the usual five years. It also means that a minister is expected to preach in other churches in the circuit besides his or her own.

A minister usually has pastoral charge of a number of churches. The conduct of worship is therefore considerably dependent on 13,000 trained and accredited Local Preachers, and the Circuit Plan is an indispensable feature of Methodist life. It indicates who is planned to take Sunday services in each church, and may include a circuit directory with other information.

A probationer minister (i.e. an ordinand) can only celebrate Holy Communion by authorisation of the Conference. Lay persons may also be authorised to celebrate in circumstances where there would otherwise be deprivation. Except for such cases of pastoral necessity the celebration of Holy Communion is reserved for the ordained ministry.

The Methodist Church was the first to make constitutional provision for ministers of other denominations whose ministries are recognised to serve as Methodist ministers. The Conference by a Standing Vote each year accords them "Recognised and Regarded" or "Authorised" status, which gives them the privileges and responsibilities of ministry and places them under Methodist discipline.

Worship

The 'hymn sandwich' remains normative, i.e. a service without resort to a printed liturgy. The minister or local preacher has considerable freedom in devising its shape and content, although there are often local conventions to be followed, for example the place of children in the service, and the involvement of members of the congregation in the reading of lessons. The sermon is still given priority. Many churches and preachers now observe the Lectionary to be found in the Methodist Service Book. "Methodism was born in song" and hymnody continues to be a vital element in worship and to be a foremost means by which Methodists express their faith and experience.

There are no regulations regarding the dress of ministers or local preachers. Ministers may wear cassock and gown, some with hood or scarf, but a preaching gown or a plain suit are still common.

Baptism and Confirmation

Christian parents are regarded as being under solemn obligation to present

80

their children for baptism, which is regarded as an unrepeatable act. Baptism is normally administered in the context of public worship, following the rite in the Methodist Service Book. In infant baptism much weight is given to the promises made by the congregation and the parents; godparents (called sponsors) are not essential, but when present are asked to promise to "support these parents in the Christian upbringing of this child". A candle is often presented after a baptism.

Confirmation or reception into full membership follows, usually for those of mature age, and may include one or both of two symbolic acts derived from the New Testament – the laying on of hands and the right hand of fellowship. The local minister usually presides and confirms. The names of those confirmed are placed on the church membership roll and are transferred to another church on removal to another area. An annual ticket of membership is provided.

The annual Covenant Service is a prized treasure initiated by John Wesley, providing a means for rededication and renewal of membership pledges.

Eucharist

In urban churches Holy Communion may be celebrated on one Sunday morning and one Sunday evening each month, but less often in rural areas. There has been a noticeable revival of eucharistic worship in recent years, and it is now no longer added to the "main" service. The tradition of the "open table" is still valued. The rite in the Methodist Service Book which contains those services authorised by the Conference, is usually used, but some churches prefer a non-liturgical service on occasions. The minister may decide how the service is to be conducted, position at the Communion table, etc., but he or she will be sensitive to local traditions. It is usual for a whole row or "table" of communicants to wait and to be dismissed together before returning to their seats. Bread and unfermented wine are used, and individual glasses are still the general rule. Any remaining elements are "disposed of reverently".

Sensitivities

There is still some suspicion of hierarchical forms of leadership in some quarters in Methodism 'Bishop', 'priest' and 'altar' continue to be terms that are held in suspicion by some. Minister' is preferred to 'Clergyman'.

Methodists remain proud of their own form of democratic process and their Connexional system, enabling the strong to help the weak.

The social conscience characteristic of earlier Methodism continues to be reflected in attitudes towards alcohol and gambling on Methodist

81

premises, and an active concern about a wide range of social and political issues. Methodists do not always take kindly to being described as a gathered church; something of the spirit of Wesley who said 'The World is my parish' continues to be expressed in an active concern for the whole community in which each church is called to be a missionary presence.

Where Methodists are in minority partnerships with Anglicans the latter need to be aware of the fear of absorption which is often present, as Methodists may need to be in the case of URC or Baptist partners.

Bibliography

Methodists and LEPs
Guidelines on Recognised and Regarded and Authorised Status for Ministers of Other Churches

Standing Orders are found in:
The Constitutional Discipline and Practice of the Methodist Church.

Further information from the Sub-Committee for Local Ecumenical Development – The Rev. Keith Reed, 25 Marylebone Road, London NW1 5JR. Tel: 0171 486 5502

4: The Roman Catholic Church
by Michael Jackson

Two things ought to be said by way of preface to what follows. First, the Roman Catholic Church in England is a full member of Churches Together in England and the Council of Churches for Britain and Ireland. Catholics are fully committed to ecumenism. The second thing is, of course, that the Catholic Church's ecumenical experience is not static. It is developing, but not necessarily uniformly in every part of the country.

Decision Making

The Roman Catholic Church is not a national church. The Catholic dioceses in England belong to a Bishops' Conference that also includes Wales. Furthermore, all Roman Catholic bishops form an international, worldwide college of bishops, whose head is the Pope. This means that some of the decisions of the English and Welsh Catholic bishops are taken in consultation with the Pope and his offices in the Vatican. The laws and disciplines which promote order and support growth in the Roman Catholic Church are encoded in the 1983 Code of Canon Law. This provides a general law for the whole Roman Catholic Church. In it there is provision for certain decisions to be made by a local bishop or by a bishops' conference (eg. on admission to Holy Communion of people who are not Roman Catholics). There is an Ecumenical Directory which gives directives for the ecumenical activities of the Catholic Church around the world. This also makes provision for certain decisions to be taken locally.

The diocese is the key structure in the Roman Catholic Church. It is sometimes called the 'local church', but is more properly called the 'particular' (as opposed to 'universal') church. A Catholic diocese has parishes and deaneries; superficially it looks similar to an Anglican diocese. Most dioceses, deaneries and parishes have pastoral councils which are consultative rather than decision making. Power for decision making lies with the bishop or the parish priest. This is important to know when, for instance, broaching the question of a local covenant.

Boundaries: Roman Catholic dioceses in England cover several counties and so are much larger in area than Anglican dioceses. Catholic bishops may be involved in several sponsoring bodies or ecumenical councils; some bishops appoint ecumenical advisors to assist them. Every Catholic diocese has at least one ecumenical commission, or ecumenical advisors. Similarly, Catholic parishes tend to be geographically large. We are all too familiar with the awkwardness that this mismatch of boundaries causes ecumenically.

Ministry

The Roman Catholic Church believes that, in the first place, people are baptised into the Christian ministry. It also believes that there is an ordained ministry which is given as a special grace to individuals for service in church. Recently there have been significant developments in the Catholic Church's approach to the ministry of lay people, who are now much more involved in the lives of their parishes.For example, certain lay people, are commissioned by the diocesan bishop as ministers to assist in the administration of Holy Communion. There has also been a significant development in the ministry of the permanent diaconate. Roman Catholics understand ministry to be wider than the ministry of the clergy.

Worship

At the heart of Roman Catholic worship lies the Eucharist, the Mass, which Catholics hold to be the source and summit of the church's life. So important is it to some that they attend Mass every day. It is a law of the church that Catholics attend Mass every Sunday.

Recent years have seen a number of developments in the prayer and devotional life of Catholics, developments which open up possibilities for greater ecumenical sharing in prayer. The Charismatic Renewal in the 60s and 70s led to prayer groups being formed in many parishes. A significant number of these are ecumenical. Some traditional Catholic devotional practices have declined. Nowadays in some parishes the Divine Office is recited. This scriptural prayer based on the psalms used to be thought of as the prayer of priests, monks and nuns. It is now known as the 'Prayer of the Church' and all Catholics are encouraged to use this form of prayer. Parts of it are not unlike Anglican Matins and Evensong.

Roman Catholic discipline concerning Holy Communion on occasion causes ecumenical difficulties. Roman Catholic teaching emphasises the close connection between Eucharist and Church. In consequence, Roman Catholics are not allowed to receive communion at the eucharistic services of most of their fellow Christians, nor are they allowed, as a general rule, to admit to Holy Communion people who are not Catholic. There are exceptions, of course, but most of these concern individuals and do not affect local ecumenical situations. It is unlikely that this discipline will change in the near future.

Baptism and Confirmation

The issue here is initiation and church membership. The Roman Catholic Church regard Baptism, Confirmation and Eucharist as the three sacraments of initiation: one's membership of the church is incomplete until all three sacraments have been received. The Catholic Church baptises adults and infants. Adult initiation follows the order, baptism, confirmation and eucharist. After infant baptism the order is normally baptism, Holy Communion (about the age of eight) and confirmation (in the teens). The Catholic Church recognises baptism when administered with the pouring of water and the invocation of the Holy Trinity.

There is occasionally call for ecumenical celebrations of these sacraments. This is often found to be quite difficult, largely because of the intimate connection between these sacraments and the church, a connection which Roman Catholics are loath to obscure in any way. Whilst joint celebrations of baptism do take place they are not frequent; simultaneous or parallel celebration of confirmation and eucharist are even less frequent. Support for such celebrations is not widespread. There is no provision for them in Canon Law or the official liturgical books of the Catholic Church. Notwithstanding this, a few priests and bishops have taken part in them. It is an area of great sensitivity.

Communion

See mainly under 3 above 'worship'.

Sensitivities

On Worship:

The official worship of the Roman Catholic Church is based on the liturgical year which begins on the First Sunday of Advent with preparations for the coming of Christ, and continues through the year with the main events in his life, death and resurrection and the sending of the Holy Spirit. Into this framework are built many other feasts, notably expressing the Catholic Church's sense of the communion of saints and the special place in it of Mary the Mother of the Lord. Statues, candles, the stations of the cross, the crucifix are features of Roman Catholic churches. In shared buildings difficulties can be raised by the presence or absence of some of these things. Great respect, plus a little imagination, can help overcome some of the difficulties.

On doctrine:

"Sound pastoral and ecumenical practice is based on sound theology" is one way of putting it. Catholics have a high regard for doctrine and theology as traditionally taught in the Catholic Church. They can sometimes appear to be sticky or over-insistent on this. The emphasis arises from a conviction that 'faith and order' divisions must be overcome for the unity of the Church to be real and true.

Resourcing Ecumenism:

The Roman Catholic Church is a very large community. Some therefore think that it is a very wealthy community. This is not the case – at least in England, where the Catholic Community is very heavily committed to a programme of Catholic education in schools and colleges. Resources are drawn from parishes and dioceses for this apostolate. Every parish priest will tell you how much he has to pay into the diocesan central development fund. He is no better off than you! But you can and should press the local Catholics and their bishop to constantly review their priorities in the light of the ecumenical commitments they have made. And expect them to do the same to you in return.

Mixed Marriages:

In the last twenty years there has been some change in the attitude of the Catholic Church towards marriages between Catholics and other

Christians. Some 70% of marriages involving Catholics in England are 'mixed marriages' – mostly with Anglicans and Methodists. The current attitude, as expressed in the Directory on Mixed Marriages (1990), is much more positive and ecumenical. The commitment of the Catholic to preserve and promote the Catholic faith remains, together with a promise (made by the Catholic), "I sincerely undertake that I will do all that I can within the unity of our partnership to have all the children of our marriage baptised and brought up in the Catholic Church."

The issues concerning Holy Communion remain at their most poignant in this setting, especially in those marriages where the spouses have a strong commitment to their faith.

Further information from your local Catholic parish priest who will be able to tell you the name of the bishop's advisor on ecumenical matters. The Secretary of the Committee for Christian Unity of the Catholic Bishops' Conference will also help (38-40 Eccleston Square, London SW1V 1PD. Tel: 0171-834 5612).

5: The United Reformed Church
by Peter Poulter

Decision Making

The United Reformed Church is a recent union of three churches with distinct patterns of structure and practice – the Congregational Church and Presbyterian Church of England in 1972, and the Churches of Christ in 1981. Local congregations frequently share some of the experience of LEPs in that individual members will have grown up with an unequal mix of the traditions and sensibilities of the three churches. Thus the variety of expectation and approach may well be greater than in most other churches.

Authority and care are exercised by the General Assembly (national), Provincial Synods and District Councils. The District Council has the responsibility to enquire pastorally into the situation of each local church under its oversight at least every five years – the Quinquennial visitation. In the case of some LEPs Council will delegate this to a sponsoring body.

In each local church elders share responsibility with the minister for regular pastoral care of the membership and, in conjunction with the church meeting, lead and direct the life of the congregation. Elders are lay people, elected by the church meeting and ordained for life by the local minister to specific pastoral and managerial responsibilities in the local congregation and in the councils of the church. Among all URC members there is a strong expectation of lay involvement in decision making at all levels.

Ministry

The URC ordains both men and women to the ministry of Word and Sacraments. Most ministers are full-time stipendiary ministers but an increasing number of non-stipendiary Auxiliary Ministers are now serving in local churches, chaplaincies and a variety of less formally structured pastoral settings.

Worship

Worship in the URC represents the same anomaly as in other Free Churches – a proud insistence on freedom from the restrictions of a set order, printed and prescribed, alongside a fairly restricted expectation of the structure and content of the normal service. This normal service is basically the read and preached word set in the context of hymns and prayers with great emphasis laid on biblical proclamation. The response of the people is usually expressed through the hymns. There is a strong tradition of metrical psalms especially in the former Presbyterian strand of the church, but little of sung psalms or canticles. Many members of most congregations will be happy with a service entirely conducted by the minister, but there is an increasing acceptance and expectation of opportunity for congregational participation and response that is more than token or ritual. Ministerial dress may vary from lounge suit and tie to cassock, bands, hood, gown and even occasionally coloured stole. Generally it involves clerical collar and gown with either suit or cassock. Some ministers may wear an alb for Holy Communion, but this is rare.

Baptism and Confirmation

Baptism in the URC was originally infant baptism, frequently observing the Reformed tradition of baptising only the children of church members. Since 1981 and the Union with the Churches of Christ, both adult and infant baptism have been practised – along with the undertaking that the circumstances of infant baptism should not be such as to minimise the significance of the rite. All traditions in the URC regard baptism as an unrepeatable act but special provisions are contained in the Scheme of Union for pastoral reconciliation in the event where 'differences of conviction within the one Church result in personal conflict of conscience'. No-one is required to administer nor submit to a form of baptism to which he/she has a conscientious objection.

Church membership/confirmation usually involves people of mature age – rarely under about 16. Reception is usually by a local minister or a senior elder in the church. The emphasis is on profession and commitment recognised and celebrated in a local relationship.

Communion

Holy Communion is central to the life of the church, but this is expressed in different ways. The Presbyterian tradition is of quarterly communion, the Churches of Christ of weekly and the Congregationalists somewhere in between. Presidency is normally by an ordained minister or an elder authorised to officiate in case of pastoral necessity. Communion is in both kinds, using leavened bread and (usually) unfermented wine of various sorts. The elements are taken to the seated members by the elders. Generally wine in served in small glasses, but LEPs may find use of both glasses and chalice, or chalice alone. There is a traditional invitation to 'all who love and acknowledge the lordship of Christ'. In practice this generally means people of a mature age and often only church members participate; there is, however, a growing and animated discussion in the URC about the place of children at communion. The bread and wine may be consumed by each person as and when it is distributed or by all together when the whole company has been served; local patterns vary.

Further information from Rev. Sheila Maxey, URC, 86 Tavistock Place, London WC1H 9RT. Tel: 0171 916 2020.

APPENDIX 2

Working Together in the New Ecumenical Instruments : Suggested Rules of Good Practice

One of the fundamental objects of the new ecumenical instruments is to enable the churches to work increasingly closely together on matters of shared concern. This is intended to go beyond friendly co-operation to, as the Swanwick declaration of 4th September 1987 put it, "clear commitment to each other, in search of the unity for which Christ prayed and in common evangelism and service of the world". *(Churches Together in Pilgrimage*, p. 7f).

As a general principle, work is no longer to be done by the ecumenical instruments on behalf of the churches, but by the member churches with and for one another. A major role of the ecumenical instruments is to enable the churches to act together – by bringing together people in the churches with common interests, acting as a channel for the exchange of information, etc.

If the member churches are to work together effectively in this way, certain ground rules need to be agreed among them and followed within the individual member churches. Following ecumenical discussion, this note offers some draft ground rules of good practice.

1. **Member churches should be ready to share their own vision of the issues which are important and their own programmes of work with the officers of the ecumenical instruments and with one another.**

    This is not an invitation to member churches to deluge one another with paper. They should, however, inform the relevant co-ordinating secretary in the Council of Churches for Britain and Ireland or officer in Churches Together in England of work projected or underway and share information about it with the relevant network, commission, co-ordinating group or agency.

    Work at intermediate (county or metropolitan area) level may be as interesting as work at national level in this context. The Field Officers of Churches Together in England have a role in this as well as the officers of the churches.

Among the key tasks of the officers of the new instruments are

- to ensure that networks, groups, commissions and agencies are established bringing together people in the churches with shared interests;
- to map out the work underway in the different member churches. Member churches can themselves help by mapping out the work, including ecumenical work, in which they are engaged;
- to act as a repository of information on work done or in progress within member churches.

2. **When considering embarking on new items of work, or reviewing existing areas of work, member churches should ask themselves whether the principles of working set out in *Churches Together in Pilgrimage* and described above are adequately embodied in the way they propose to proceed.**

    At the Faith and Order Conference at Lund in Sweden in 1952 the participants asked the member churches "whether they should not act together in all matters except those in which deep differences of conviction compel them to act separately". This question should be constantly before our churches as they consider all their activities. Of course there may be circumstances in which it makes sense to establish a working party or other group on a denominational basis. But many issues are of common interest to the churches, and can be addressed more efficiently and comprehensively if the work is done ecumenically.

    When member churches are reviewing existing work or considering new work they should therefore share their proposals for action with other member churches through the relevant ecumenical body. In this way ecumenical considerations should become not an additional factor to be considered at the end of a project, but part of the very thinking about it from its inception, and also a regular factor in any review of existing work.

3. **Member churches should take into account priorities established ecumenically when considering their own internal priorities for work.**

    All member churches and the new ecumenical instruments have limited resources. Choices have to be made about how those resources are to be used.

    Priorities for the Council of Churches for Britain and Ireland are decided by member churches through the Church Representatives Meeting, noting advice from the Steering Committee. Priorities for Churches Together in England are decided by the member churches through the Enabling Group, which includes representation both of the intermediate bodies (county or metropolitan area ecumenical councils) and of the member churches.

Each member church has its own different structure of authority through which decisions about priorities are taken.

There is no neat way in which the processes of establishing priorities within individual member churches and collectively within the new ecumenical instruments can be brought together. Denominational responsibilities and structures vary, and cannot easily be aligned. The important thing is that there should be a continuing process of dialogue – through representative bodies groups, commissions, agencies, networks, etc. – so that decisions about priorites in each context are informed by thinking and views expressed in the other. It is also important that churches should be sensitive to the possibility of the gradual alignment of structures where that would pose no substantial threat to their particular structure of authority.

The principles laid down in the report *'Churches Together in Pilgrimage'*, and charity itself, demand that where one church or group of churches has a priority which requires action from other churches, the other churches take this very seriously.

4. **Member churches should be on the look-out for opportunities to share resources with one another by offering to undertake particular pieces of work.**

    The Church Representatives Meeting or Enabling Group may ask member churches to undertake particular pieces of work on behalf of others. But individual churches also need to be on the look-out for opportunities to offer their work in the service of all.

    On the whole, given the limited resources of member churches, it makes sense to co-operate/share resources wherever possible. In that way, small contributions can together add up to a useful sum, and the smaller churches can be helped by the larger. Proposals for ecumenical sharing need to be cleared through the new instruments. They should:

    ●   be agreed within the member church making the proposal;
    ●   be agreed by the other member churches;
    ●   include a clear understanding about how the shared arrange-

ment is to work, what contributions are expected from each participating church, and how accountability to the member churches is to be ensured.

5. **Member churches should consider carefully the development of methods of working which further ecumenical co-operation.**
    Methods of working which are normal in some churches may not help in achieving the involvement of other churches in a piece of work which is to be taken forward ecumenically. For example, it is difficult for those churches which lack large central staffs to participate in meetings during normal working hours, since they often have to rely on volunteers to represent them.

    There may also be a need to think imaginatively about how reports developed ecumenically are processed within the member churches. For example, an ecumenical working group may prepare a draft of conclusions and recommendations resulting from a piece of work, but it may help the handling and acceptance of a particular report if its conclusions and recommendations are put in final form by the board or committee which has direct responsibility for the subject within each member church.

    There may also be ways for the churches to satisfy the needs of their own denominational networks as well as the need for ecumenical co-operation without adding extra meetings. For example it may be possible for the networks of all the churches in a particular field to meet at the same time, and to devote some of the meeting to separate denominational concerns in denominational groups, and some of the meeting to shared concerns in a plenary gathering.

6. **The Enabling Group of Churches Together in England and member churches will need to think carefully about what work is to be done under the auspices of Churches Together in England and what under the auspices of the Council of Churches for Britain and Ireland.**
    The division of responsibility between the Council of Churches for Britain and Ireland and Churches Together in England is not yet clear. It will need to be worked out in careful dialogue between the two. In that dialogue, the English churches will need to be alive to the sensitivities of the Scottish, Welsh and Irish ecumenical bodies when proposing joint action under the auspices of the Council of Churches for Britain and Ireland. At the same time it is in the interest of all churches to avoid duplication wherever it is possible

and sensible to do so, and to ensure that the results of work by member churches are shared as widely within the new instruments as possible.

Martin Reardon
on behalf of the Enabling Group
CTE, December 1991

APPENDIX 3

The Convenant of Churches Together in Dronfield and District

1. We, the members of: Apperknowle Methodist Church; Coal Aston Methodist Church; Coal Aston Wesleyan Reform Church; Church of the Holy Spirit; Dronfield Baptist Church; Dronfield Methodist Free Church (Wesleyan Reform Union); Dronfield Parish Church; Dronfield Woodhouse Methodist Church; Hill Top United Reformed Church; Oaks Christian Fellowship; St Andrew's Community Church; St Mary's United Church, Unstone; St Paul's Methodist Church; St Philip's Church, Holmesdale; St Swithin's Church, Holmesfield,

    reaffirm our belief that the visible unity of the life and mission of all Christ's people is the will of God; but this does not mean uniformity but legitimate diversity.

2. We acknowledge the authority of Scripture and the truth of the Apostles' Creed and in so doing, we affirm our faith in God as Father who is the Creator, in Jesus Christ as Lord and Saviour, and in the Holy Spirit who continues God's work in the world today.

3. We rejoice in our traditions but recognise that our diversity can occasion unnecessary divisions which are a hindrance to mission. We repent all that is sinful in our past histories and present attitudes.

4. We therefore make this commitment to God and to each other and we covenant to seek that visible unity, even though in our pilgrimage together we cannot foresee the form it will eventually take.

5. We commit ourselves and our churches:

    a. to move through co-operation to clear commitment to each other, in search of the unity for which Christ prayed and in common evangelism and service to the world.

b. to engage in joint worship, prayer and study so that we may know and value each other and seek God's will for His people.

c. to work together in pastoral, social and evangelistic outreach into our community.

d. to publicise and promote our Church life and worship by joint means wherever possible.

e. to develop a Ministerial Team for regular prayer, study, consultation and appropriate action.

f. to create 'Churches Together in Dronfield and District' made up of an Assembly to the Ministerial Team and representatives from all participating churches. This Assembly will have power and finance to act on those matters which the individual churches have authorised it to carry out on their behalf.

g. to ensure that all Ministerial appointments, although made by each denomination, are made with such consultation with the Ministerial Team as is reasonably possible, consonant with denominational procedures.

APPENDIX 4

Text of Canons B43 and B44 of the Church of England

Canon B43 of Relations with other Churches

1 (1) A minister or lay person who is a member in good standing of a Church to which this Canon applies and is a baptised person may, subject to the provisions of this Canon, be invited to perform all or any of the following duties:

a) to say or sing Morning or Evening Prayer or the Litany;
b) to read the Holy Scriptures at any service;
c) to preach at any service;
d) to lead the Intercessions at the Holy Communion and to lead prayers at other services;
e) to assist at Baptism or the Solemnisation of Matrimony or conduct a Funeral Service;
f) to assist in the distribution of the holy sacrament of the Lord's Supper to the people at the Holy Communion;

if the minister or lay person is authorised to perform a similar duty in his or her own Church.

(2) An invitation to perform in a parish church or other place of worship in the parish any of the duties mentioned in sub-paragraph (1) above, other than duties in connection with a service or ordination or confirmation, may be given only by the incumbent and may be given only if

a) in the case of:

i) any duty mentioned in sub-paragraph (1)(f) above or,
ii) any duty mentioned in sub-paragraph (1)(a), (c) or (e) above, which is to be performed on a regular basis,

the approval of the bishop has been obtained; and

b) in the case of any duty mentioned in sub-paragraph (1)(e) above, the persons concerned have requested the incumbent to give the invitation; and

c) in the case of any duty mentioned in sub-paragraph (1)(a), (c) or (f) above, the approval of the parochial church council has been obtained.

(3) An invitation to perform in a parish church or other place of worship in the parish any duty in connection with a service of ordination or confirmation may be given only by the bishop and may be given only if the approval of the incumbent and the parochial church council has been obtained.

(4) Sub-paragraphs (2) and (3) above shall apply in relation to an invitation to perform in a cathedral church any of the duties mentioned in sub-paragraph (1) above subject to the following modifications:

a) for any reference to the incumbent there shall be substituted –

i) in the case of a dean and chapter cathedral, the dean and chapter, and
ii) in the case of a parish church cathedral, the cathedral chapter, and

b) the provisions relating to the approval of the parochial church council shall not apply.

2 Notwithstanding any provision of any Canon, a bishop who receives from a person authorised by a Church to which this Canon applies an invitation to take part in a service may in the course of that service perform any duty assigned to him if –

a) the duty assigned to him is or is similar to a duty which he is authorised to perform in the Church of England; and
b) he has before accepting the invitation obtained

i) the approval of the incumbent of the parish in which the service is to take place, and
ii) in the case of an invitation to take part in a service in another diocese, the approval of the bishop of that diocese, and
iii) in the case of an invitation to take part in the ordination or consecration of a minister of a hurch to which this Canon applies, to take part in a service of confirmation or to preside at the Holy Communion, the approval of the archbishop of the province.

3   Notwithstanding any provision of any Canon, a priest or deacon of the Church of England who receives from a person authorised by a Church to which this Canon applies an invitation to take part in a service may in the course of that service perform any duty assigned to him if –

a)   the duty assigned to him is or is similar to a duty which he is authorised to perform in the Church of England, and

b)   he has before accepting the invitation obtained

i)   the approval of the incumbent of the parish in which the service is to take place, and

ii)   in the case of an invitation to take part in the ordination or consecration of a minister of a Church to which this Canon applies or to preside at the Holy Communion, the approval of the bishop of the diocese in which the service is to take place, and

iii) in the case of an invitation to take part in any service on a regular basis, the approval of both the bishop of the diocese and the parochial church council of the parish in which the service is to take place.

4   In the case of an invitation to preside at the Holy Communion, the archbishop shall not give his approval under paragraph 2 above and the bishop shall not give his approval under paragraph 3 above unless the archbishop or the bishop, as the case may be, is satisfied that there are special circumstances which justify acceptance of the invitation and that the rite and the elements to be used are not contrary to, nor indicative of any departure from, the doctrine of the Church of England in any essential matter.

5   A bishop or priest who has accepted an invitation to take part in the ordination or consecration of a minister of a Church to which this Canon applies may not, by the laying on of hands or otherwise, do any act which is a sign of the conferring of Holy Orders, unless that Church is an episcopal Church with which the Church of England has established intercommunion.

6   Notwithstanding any provision of any Canon, a deaconess, lay worker or reader of the Church of England who receives from a person authorised by a Church to which this Canon applies an

invitation to take part in a service may in the course of that service perform any duty assigned to him or her if –

a)   the duty so assigned is or is similar to a duty which he or she is authorised to perform in the Church of England; and

b)   he or she has before accepting the invitation obtained the approval of the incumbent of the parish in which the service is to take place and also, in the case of an invitation to take part in a service on a regular basis, the approval of both the bishop of the diocese and the parochial church council of that parish.

7   Where, on an application under paragraph 3 or 6 above for the approval of an incumbent, that approval is withheld, the applicant may appeal to the bishop of the diocese in which the service is to take place and if, after considering the views of the applicant and the incumbent, the bishop determines that approval has been unreasonably withheld, the bishop may authorise the applicant to take part in the service in question and where the bishop so determines the bishop shall inform the incumbent in writing of the reasons for that determination.

8   Where the approval of the parochial church council is required for the giving or accepting of an invitation under the preceding provisions of this Canon, that approval may be given in respect of the performance of such duties as may be specified in the approval by such person or persons, or such class of persons, as may be so specified and may either be given generally for an unlimited period or given subject to such limitations, whether as to duration or occasion, as may be so specified.

9   The incumbent of a parish may, with the approval of the parochial church council and the bishop of the diocese, invite members of another Church to which this Canon applies to take part in joint worship with the Church of England or to use a church in the parish for worship in accordance with the forms of service and practice of that other Church on such occasions as may be specified in the approval given by the bishop.

10   The dean and chapter or the cathedral chapter of any cathedral church may with the approval of the bishop of the diocese invite

members of another church to which this Canon applies to take part in joint worship with the Church of England, or to use the cathedral church for worship in accordance with the forms of service and practice of that other Church, on such occasions as may be specified in the approval given by the bishop.

11   Any approval required by this Canon to be obtained from a bishop or archbishop shall be in writing and shall be given in accordance with such directions as may from time to time be given by the House of Bishops of the General Synod.

12 (1) This Canon applies to every Church to which the Church of England (Ecumenical Relations) Measure 1988 applies.

   (2) In this Canon 'incumbent', in relation to a parish, includes –

   a)   in a case where the benefice concerned is vacant (and paragraph (b) below does not apply) the rural dean and
   b)   in a case where a suspension period (within the meaning of the Pastoral Measure 1983) applies to the benefice concerned, the priest-in-charge, and
   c)   in a case where a special cure of souls in respect of the parish has been assigned to a vicar in a team ministry by a scheme under the Pastoral Measure 1983 or by his licence from the bishop, that vicar, and 'place of worship' means a building or part of a building licensed for public worship.

Canon B44 of Local Ecumenical Projects

1 (1) The bishop of a diocese may enter into an agreement with the appropriate authority of each participating Church with regard to the participation of the Church of England in a local ecumenical project established or to be established for an area comprising any parish in his diocese (not being the parish of a cathedral church) or part of such a parish.

   (2) Where the area of a local ecumenical project is extended so as to include a parish which was not previously included (not being the parish of a cathedral church) or to include part of such a parish, the Church of England shall not participate in the project in respect of that parish or part of a parish unless the bishop of the diocese has agreed thereto.

(3) A bishop shall not enter into any agreement under sub-paragraph (1) or (2) above as respects any parish or part of a parish unless the participation of the Church of England in the project in respect of the parish concerned has been approved –

a) by the incumbent of that parish; and

b) by 75% of those present and voting at a meeting of the parochial church council of that parish; and

c) by either the annual parochial church meeting or a special parochial church meeting of that parish; and

d) by the diocesan pastoral committee after consultation with the deanery synod concerned or the standing committee of that synod.

2 (1) Any agreement made under paragraph 1(1) above shall have effect for such period of not more than seven years as may be specified therein, but may from time to time be extended by an agreement made by the bishop of the diocese concerned for such further period of not more than seven years as may be specified in that later agreement.

(2) Where a local ecumenical project is amended so as to include a Church which was not previously participating in the project, or to include an additional congregation of a participating Church, the Church of England shall not continue to participate in that project unless the bishop of the diocese concerned has agreed to that amendment or, if the area of the project comprises parishes or part of parishes in more than one diocese, the bishops of those dioceses have so agreed.

(3) A bishop of a diocese shall not make any agreement under sub-paragraph (1) or (2) above unless he has obtained the consent of

a) the incumbent of each parish concerned, and

b) each parochial church council concerned, and

c) the diocesan pastoral committee.

3 (1) A bishop may at any time revoke any agreement made under the foregoing provisions of this Canon after consultation with the appropriate authority of each participating Church, each parochial church council concerned and the diocesan pastoral committee.

(2) Any agreement made under the foregoing provisions of this Canon shall be in writing.

4 (1)   A bishop who has given his agreement to participation in a local ecumenical project under the foregoing provisions of this Canon may by an instrument* in writing made after consultation with the parochial church council of each parish or part of a parish in the area of the project,

* A precedent of an instrument under Canon B44 is available separately (*Draft Instrument under Canon B44, General Synod 1989*).

a)   make special provision as to the ministry in that area of clerks in Holy Orders, deaconesses, lay workers and readers beneficed in or licensed to any parish wholly or partly in that area;

b)   exercise in relation to that area his powers under paragraph 2 of Canon B11, paragraph 1 of Canon B11A, paragraph 1 and 2 of Canon B14, Canon B40 and Canon B43;

c)   authorise ministers of any other participating Church with the goodwill of the persons concerned to baptise in a place of worship of the Church of England in that area in accordance with a rite authorised by any participating Church;

d)   authorise a priest of the Church of England to preside in that area at a service of Holy Communion in accordance with a rite authorised by any other participating Church;

e)   make provision for the holding in that area of joint services with any other participating Church, including services of baptism and confirmation;

f)   authorise the holding, in a place of worship of the Church of England in that area, of services of Holy Communion presided over by a minister of any other participating Church.

(2)   A bishop shall not by any instrument made under this paragraph authorise any rite to be used in any service mentioned in sub-paragraph (1)(d), (e) or (f) above unless he is satisfied that the rite and the elements to be used are not contrary to, nor indicative of any departure from, the doctrine of the Church of England in any essential matter.

(3)   Where the holding of a service of Holy Communion is authorised under sub-paragraph (1)(f) above –

a)   notice of the holding of any such service shall, so far as practicable, be given upon the Sunday immediately preceding

103

with an indication of the rite to be used and the Church to which the minister who is to preside thereat belongs; and

b)   no such service, notwithstanding that the form of service used may follow a form authorised under Canon B1 or a form substantially similar thereto, shall be held out or taken to be a celebration of the Holy Communion according to the use of the Church of England;

c)   no portion of the bread and wine consecrated at any such service shall be carried out of the church in accordance with the provisions of Canon B37(2) except at the express wish of the individual sick communicant, in which case this shall be done either during or immediately after the service, or as soon as practicable on the same day.

(4)   An instrument made under this paragraph with respect to any local ecumenical project may be amended or revoked by a subsequent instrument made after consultation with the parochial church council of each parish which is in, or part of which is in, the area of that project.

5   Before exercising his powers under paragraph 4 above in relation to any local ecumenical project the bishop shall consult the authorities of the other participating Churches, and he shall so exercise those powers as to ensure that public worship according to the rites of the Church of England is maintained with reasonable frequency in a parish which is in, or part of which is in, the area of the project and in particular that a service of Holy Communion according to the rites of the Church of England or by an episcopally ordained priest in a Church whose Orders are recognised and accepted by the Church of England shall be celebrated at least on Christmas Day, Ash Wednesday, Easter Day, Ascension Day and Pentecost.

6 (1)   Where a local ecumenical project is established or is to be established for an area in which a cathedral church is situated, the bishop of the diocese may, after consultation with the dean and chapter or cathedral chapter of that cathedral church and after such other consultation as he considers appropriate, enter into an agreement with the appropriate authority of each participating Church with regard to the participation of that cathedral church in the project.

(2)   The provisions of paragraphs 2 to 4 above shall apply in relation to an agreement made or project participated in by virtue of sub-paragraph (1) above subject to the following modifications –

    a)   sub-paragraph (3) of paragraph 3 shall not apply but the bishop before making an agreement under sub-paragraph (1) or (2) of that paragraph with respect to a project in which a cathedral church is participating shall consult the dean and chapter or cathedral chapter of that cathedral church;

    b)   in paragraph 3(1) for the reference to each parochial church council concerned and the diocesan pastoral committee there shall be substituted a reference to the dean and chapter or cathedral chapter of the cathedral church concerned;

    c)   in paragraph 4 for the reference in sub-paragraphs (1) and (4) to the parochial church council of each parish or part of a parish in the area of the project there shall be substituted a reference to the dean or chapter or cathedral chapter of the cathedral church concerned and for the reference in sub-paragraph (1)(a) to clerks in Holy Orders, deaconesses, lay workers and readers beneficed or licensed to any parish wholly or partly in the area there shall be substituted a reference to clerks in Holy Orders, deaconesses, lay workers and readers ministering in or licensed to the cathedral church concerned; and

    d)   before exercising his powers under paragraph 4 in relation to a project participated in by virtue of sub-paragraph (1) above the bishop shall consult the authorities of the other participating Churches.

(3)   Nothing in this paragraph shall affect the requirements of Canon B10 or B13 regarding services in cathedral churches.

7 (1)   Where a local ecumenical project is established or to be established for an institution and a clerk in Holy Orders is licensed under section 2 of the Extra-Parochial Ministry Measure 1967 in respect of that institution, the bishop of the diocese may, after such consultation as he considers appropriate, enter into an agreement with the appropriate authority of each participating Church with regard to the participation of the Church of England in that project.

(2)   A bishop shall not enter into an agreement under sub-paragraph (1) above as respects any institution unless the participation of the

Church of England in the project concerned has been approved by the diocesan pastoral committee.

(3)   The provisions of paragraphs 2 to 5 above shall, so far as applicable, apply in relation to an agreement made or project participated in by virtue of this paragraph as they apply in relation to an agreement made or project participated in by virtue of paragraph 1 above, subject to the following modifications –

a)   for any reference to the area of the project there shall be substituted a reference to the institution concerned;

b)   for the reference to clerks in Holy Orders, deaconesses, lay workers and readers beneficed in or licensed in respect of the institution concerned; and

c)   any reference to an incumbent or to a parochial church council shall be omitted.

8   The powers of a bishop under this Canon may be exercised only in respect of a local ecumenical project in which every other Church participating in the project is a Church to which the Church of England (Ecumenical Relations) Measure 1988 applies.

9   In this Canon –

'incumbent', in relation to a parish, includes –

a)   in a case where the benefice concerned is vacant (and paragraph (b) below does not apply), the rural dean, and

b)   in a case where a suspension period (within the meaning of the Pastoral Measure 1983) applies to the benefice concerned, the priest-in-charge, and

c)   in a case where a special cure of souls in respect of the parish has been assigned to a vicar in a team ministry by a scheme under the Pastoral Measure 1983 or by his licence from the bishop, that vicar;

'local ecumenical project' has the same meaning as in the Church of England (Ecumenical Relations) Measure 1988;

'minister', in relation to any other participating Church, means any person ordained to the ministry of the Word and Sacraments;

'participating Church', in relation to a local ecumenical project, means a Church which is participating in that project.

106

APPENDIX 5

Baptist/Methodist Agreement on Baptismal Policy within Local Ecumenical Projects

Finalised after long consultation between the Baptist Union Advisory Committee on Church Relations and the Methodist Church Ecumenical Committee.

A. We recognise the necessity of:

i) Maintaining the integrity of both Methodist and Baptist understandings and practice of baptism;
ii) Having a flexible and sensitive approach in this very delicate area;
iii) Maintaining and developing good relationships and unity within the congregations of the sharing churches.

B. We note that:

i) It is the practice of the Methodist Church to baptise infants and to confirm them on confession of faith or, when infant baptism has not occurred, to baptise and confirm believers. In both cases these services make provision for pouring, sprinkling or immersion in water.
ii) It is the practice in Baptist churches to hold a service for infants and their parents (variously known as "The Dedication Service", "The Service of Infant Presentation and Blessing", "The Blessing of Infants", etc) and to administer believer's baptism on the candidate's personal profession of faith in Christ.
iii) Standing Order 800 of "The Constitutional Practice and Discipline of the Methodist Church" makes it clear that "it is contrary to the principles and usage of the Methodist Church to confer what purports to be baptism on any person known to have already been baptised at any time".

iv) Whilst welcoming "Baptism, Eucharist and Ministry" (the so-called Lima Document) as a "notable milestone in the search for sufficient theological consensus", the BUGB Council in November 1984 dismissed as wholly unacceptable in its present form the statement that, "Any practice which might be interpreted as 'rebaptism' must be avoided". In this way the Council sought to protect the freedom of an individual's "informed conscience" in matters concerning baptism and to allow for the possibility of a change of conviction here.

v) Whereas "Recognised and Regarded" (Methodist) ministers are expected to administer infant baptism in appropriate circumstances those with "Authorised" (Methodist) status have greater flexibility here. This latter category may accordingly be more acceptable to (most) Baptist ministers in Local Ecumenical Projects.

C. Procedures:

1. Since baptism, whether of believers or infants, is such an important step, any persons involved (candidates or parents of infants) should proceed with the full knowledge of all the options that are available to them. Candidates for believer's baptism and confirmation shall, wherever possible be trained together and shall thus be made aware of the teaching of both churches.

2. It shall be left to the discretion of the Baptist membership to baptise as believers any who have previously been baptised as infants in other churches. In the interests of the unity of the congregation this should not be applied to Methodist members except as provided under 4 below.

3. Whenever a Methodist member wishes to make a public confession of faith (other than through those opportunities normally provided by the services of the Methodist Church) then the Methodist Church Council shall arrange an appropriate opportunity such as The Service for the Celebration of Christian Renewal.

4. If, despite the above provision, any Methodist maintains a conviction about being baptised as a believer, this shall only be after a full consultation between (1) the candidate AND (2) the Baptist minister and Church Meeting and the Superintendent Minister and Church

Council. This consultation will, of course, be pastoral in nature and not in the way of a tribunal. In view of SO 800 such a service should not take place unless the Methodist member is willing to have his/her membership transferred to the Baptist roll.

APPENDIX 6

From the report of The Consultation on the Future of Leps, March 1994: Elements of an effective LEP

1. **Vision**
   A regular and prayerful reminder of what it means to be an LEP and to discern a clearer vision of God's purpose for it.
   eg. *How often does the LEP look at its Declaration of Intent or Covenant?*

2. **Community Involvement and Evangelism**
   Considered policies for community involvement and evangelism.
   eg. *Are the premises used by the local community? Are members of the congregation involved? Does this bring people into the worshipping community? Does it matter? Do they stay?*

3. **Decision-making**
   Appropriate decision-making structures which are sensitive to the needs of all, particularly minorities, and to the leading of the Holy Spirit.
   eg. *At whose pace does the church move?*

4. **Spirituality**
   The spiritual renewal of individual members of the congregation through the experience of different traditions within the LEP (for example, retreats, contemplative prayer, spiritual direction, healing ministry).
   eg. *How does the LEP feel about periods of silence or spontaneous prayer?*
   How does an LEP creatively encourage charismatic and other forms of spirituality?

111

5. **Worship**
Experience of the rich diversity of the different traditions. A holding in tension of regular liturgy and free worship.
eg. *Does the pattern of worship of the LEP enable all people to experience Jesus in their midst, to worship God, and to offer themselves for service?*

6. **Stewardship of Resources, including Finance**
Recognition and deployment of the LEP's resources, material, personnel, and financial.
eg. *Does the LEP support denominational outlets for mission?*

7. **Support**
Effective support from and to other local churches, the denominations and the Sponsoring Body.
eg. *Are there boundaries which cause problems for the LEP? Are the structures a help or a hindrance?*

8. **Collaborative Ministry**
A collaborative style of ministry which involves not only the clergy team but also lay people. Recognition and training of lay leadership across the denominations.
eg. *What training is lay leadership receiving?*

9. **Sacrifice, Commitment and Perseverance**
Sacrificial love which is prepared to share the pain of present divisions. Commitment perseverance and risk-taking for the sake of unity.
eg. *Does the LEP avoid painful decisions?*

10 **Variety of Gifts**
Acknowledgement of each other's gifts in mutual trust.
eg. *How does the LEP discern and use the gifts of the members of the congregation?*

11 **Prophetic Role**
Prophetic to the community, to the denominations and to the world by reconciliation and overcoming division, and by inviting denominational church structures to ask the ecumenical questions.
eg. *Does the community take the voice of the church seriously? What difference does the LEP's presence make to the circuit/deanery/district? How far does the LEP push denominational boundaries?*

APPENDIX 7

Model Constitutional Guidelines for a Joint Methodist and United Reformed Church

These are guidelines for the constitution of a local ecumenical project involving Methodist and United Reformed congregations. Not all the elements will be applicable in every case and some choices will have to be made locally with the help of the sponsoring body and denominational ecumenical officers. The constitutional systems of the two denominations are not compatible, the URC giving priority to the Church Meeting and the Methodist Church to the Church Council. Compromises have to be agreed in each situation to achieve an appropriate balance. While most clauses are open to negotiation some parts must be considered as mandatory, for example those dealing with membership discipline and property.

DECLARATION OF INTENT

.... United Reformed Church, and ....
Methodist Church, believing in one, holy, catholic and apostolic church and seeking the visible unity of the Church in worship and mission, have covenanted to work, worship and witness as one congregation under the name of .... (Methodist and United Reformed).

CONSTITUTION

1. **Name**
    The Joint Church shall be known as (specify).

2. The Joint Church shall be part of the United Reformed Church in the United Kingdom and of the Methodist Church.

3. **Sponsoring Body**
    The Joint Church shall be recognised as a local ecumenical project looking to (designate name of Sponsoring Body) for support and oversight. The Sponsoring Body shall indicate the membership and

113

terms of reference of an intermediate group or individual between the LEP and the Sponsoring Body.

4. **Baptism and Membership**

The .... joint church accepts the faith and practice of both the Methodist and United Reformed churches regarding Baptism and Confirmation.

The Church Council shall have oversight of matters concerned with membership, as under the terms of Clause 7B vii. Baptism shall be administered according to the rite and practice of either denomination or an ecumenical rite approved by the Sponsoring Body, and should be set, in normal circumstances, within an act of congregational worship.

A service of confirmation and recognition of church membership shall be administered according to the rite and practice of either denomination or an approved ecumenical rite. Preparation shall include specific denominational teaching and instruction. Those received into full membership through an act of joint confirmation shall be regarded as joint members.

There shall be a Common Roll of all members including joint members. A separate list of members shall also be kept for each denomination, joint members being included on each list. For purposes of denominational assessment the joint members shall be divided as determined by the Church Council in consultation with the Sponsoring Body. Membership discipline shall continue to be a matter for each denomination following its own procedures (note the ecumenical provision permitted under Methodist Standing Orders 567, 651 and 826A).

5. **Ministry**

The Minister of the joint church shall be invited in accordance with the practice of the United Reformed or Methodist Church as the case may be in a full consultation with the other church. The practice to be followed shall be that of the denomination from which the Minister is sought. The size and scope of his/her pastoral responsibility shall be as agreed by the Methodist Circuit and the URC District Council after consultation with the Church Council.

In the case of a URC minister his/her continuance (or otherwise) shall be reviewed after the first ..... years, and thereafter every .... years by the URC District Council, after consultation with the

Church Council and the Circuit. In the case of a Methodist Minister a review (under SOs 545-547) shall include consultation with the Church Council and URC District.

A Methodist Minister serving the joint church shall agree to abide by United Reformed Church doctrine and practice and shall give an undertaking to seek to foster good relations with both parent denominations. He/she will seek full membership of the District Council and of the Provincial Synod. A United Reformed Minister serving the joint church shall seek to be Recognised and Regarded as a Methodist minister (under Standing Orders 765 and 767), shall sign the prescribed Declaration required by the Methodist church and shall, within the Induction Service, give an undertaking to foster good relationships with both parent denominations.

When it is anticipated that a minister serving the Joint Church may leave, or before any major changes in the responsibility of the minister presently in post are considered, there shall be a meeting of a Staffing Consultative Group appointed by the Sponsoring Body.

This Group shall be responsible for the drawing up of any job description or the amending of an existing one. The procedure to be followed in appointing or re-appointing a minister shall be agreed and shall conform to the requirements of the participating denominations.

The Group shall decide from which denomination the next minister shall be sought, although normally there shall be an alternating ministry between the two denominations.

(The group shall normally consist of: The Superintendent Minister and a Circuit Steward of the Methodist Circuit, the Chairman of the Methodist District or his/her representative, 2 representatives of the URC District Council, the URC Provincial Moderator or his/her representative, 2 representatives of the LEP, and 2 representatives of the Sponsoring Body, one of whom shall chair the Group.)

6. **Worship**

Worship shall be ordered to give expression to the traditions of both denominations.

The Joint Church accepts the faith and practice of both the Methodist and United Reformed churches regarding the administration of the Lord's Supper. In arranging other services due consideration shall be given to the participation of local/lay preachers.

7. **Joint Decision Making**

A. The joint church shall assemble in Church Meeting (at least once a quarter) under the chairmanship of the minister(s), and all members on its Rolls shall be eligible to attend, speak and vote; non-members may be invited to attend but shall not vote. During a ministerial vacancy when considering an invitation/ call the Interim Moderator or the Methodist Superintendent (or their deputies) shall preside, depending on which denomination is seeking a minister.

In Church Meeting members have opportunity through discussion, responsible decision making and care for one another, to strengthen each other's faith and to foster the life and work and mission of the church. Generally the functions of Church Meeting shall be:

i) to further the Church's mission at home and abroad.

ii) to develop local ecumenical relationships.

iii) to consider matters of public concern in relation to the Christian faith

iv) to bring to the notice of the Church Council and to the wider Councils any matter for their consideration.

v) on the advice of the Church Council, to determine the number and the period of service (normally three years) of Elders/Leaders, and to elect them.

vi) to receive the report of the Church Council on all matters pertaining to membership.

vii) to adopt the annual accounts and receive other financial reports, and to make arrangements for the auditing/ checking of accounts.

viii) to receive reports and proposals from the Church Council and from representative bodies of both denominations and to authorise appropriate action.

ix) to make such appointments of offices within the joint church and to the wider councils of the churches and to other representative groups as may be deemed appropriate.

x) (where a building is vested in URC) to make arrangements for the proper maintenance of the building (under the terms of the Sharing Agreement)
OR (where the building is vested in the Methodist Church) to receive a property report from the Church

Council and to offer such advice as may be appropriate.

xi) to make arrangements for the general oversight of all the financial responsibilities of the joint church on the recommendation of the Church Council.

xii) to work as a constituent part of the .... Methodist Circuit and the .... District Council.

B. The joint church shall have a Church Council meeting at least once a quarter under the chairmanship of the minister(s). It shall be composed of Elders/Leaders who shall combine the functions of URC Elders and Methodist Stewards and Councillors, and a Methodist Circuit Steward (under Standing Order 614). Elders/Leaders shall share with the minister in the pastoral oversight and leadership of the local church. Some will have a group of members entrusted to their pastoral care; others may have different responsibilities in the life of the local church such as responsibilities for arrangements for Sunday worship. There shall be at least one member of the Church Council on any committee set up by the Church Meeting for the care of Property, Finance, Worship and the Sacraments, and such other matters as from time to time are deemed to be necessary. Elders/Leaders shall be elected by Church Meeting, and set apart by prayer in the context of public worship and in the presence of a representative of the URC District Council: Such setting apart shall be understood by the URC as ordination. They are inducted to serve for such limited period as the Church Meeting shall decide, and are regarded for URC purposes as Elders.

The Church Council may be given a different name where the premises are vested in the URC.

Generally the functions of the Church Council shall be:

i) to share with the minister in the pastoral oversight of the church.

ii) to see that arrangements are made so that public worship is regularly offered and the Sacraments duly administered.

iii) to be responsible for the institution and oversight of work among children and young people and of all other church organisations.

iv) to foster in the congregation concern for witness and service at home and abroad.

v) to be responsible for the day to day pastoral care, administration and outreach.

vi) to recommend to the Church Meeting the number of members of the Church Council that will be required and to make recommendations regarding the length of service (normally three years).

vii) to recommend to the Church Meeting proper arrangements for the general oversight of all financial responsibilities of the joint church.

ix) (where a building is vested in the URC) to recommend to the Church Meeting proper arrangements for the maintenance of the buildings under the terms of the Sharing Agreement.
OR (where a building is vested in the Methodist Church) to act, when constituted according to Standing Order 614, as managing trustees for the buildings and to make proper arrangements for their maintenance.

x) to advise the Church Meeting on such other committees as will facilitate the proper fulfilment of the church's worship, mission and service.

xi) to nominate a Church Secretary and Treasurer to be elected by Church Meeting, who shall then be members of the Church Council.

xii) to bring all major issues to the Church Meeting for consideration, decision and support of the church members.

xiv) to do such other things as may be necessary in pursuance of its responsibility for the common life of the church.

8. **Premises**
(Where the United Reformed and Methodist churches have entered into a Sharing Agreement under the Sharing of Church Buildings Act 1969 there shall be a Joint Council (as distinct from the Church council) as required by the Sharing of Church Buildings Act).

9. **Finance**
The joint church shall be responsible for paying through the normal denominational channels an assessment and expenses towards the costs of ministry as determined by the .... Methodist Circuit and the .... URC District Council.
   The advice of the Sponsoring Body shall be sought in determining the apportionment of costs.

118

The joint church shall be responsible for contributions which are normal in Methodist and United Reformed Churches towards denominational funds for work at home and overseas.

10. **Wider Participation**
Other churches may negotiate for participation in the project at any time, subject to the agreement of the Sponsoring Body and of the appropriate denominational authorities.

11. **Review**
The Sponsoring Body shall ensure that at least every seven years the project shall be reviewed with reference to its objectives. Normally this shall be so arranged as to fulfil the responsibilities of the URC District Council for a Quinquennial Visit and any equivalent Methodist procedures.

12. **Continuity**
The project may only be terminated with the approval of (the Sponsoring Body and) the appropriate denominational authorities.

13. Any amendment to this constitution shall require three months notice to be given to the Church Meeting and to the Church Council.
A like notice shall be given to the Superintendent Minister/ Chairman of the District of the Methodist Church, to the moderator of the Province of the United Reformed Church and to the Secretary of the Sponsoring Body. No such amendment shall be valid until it has been approved by not less than three quarters of those present and voting at a meeting of the Church Council and has received the concurrence of the said Chairman and Moderator and the approval of the appropriate denominational authorities and the Sponsoring Body.

Methodist and United Reformed Church Liaison Committee 1993

APPENDIX 8

Useful Addresses

Churches Together in England (CTE) (London Office)
Inter-Church House
35-41 Lower Marsh
London SE1 7RL
Tel : 0171 620 4444

Churches Together in England (Field Officer for South)
Baptist House
129 Broadway
Didcot
Oxon OX11 8XD
Tel: 01235 511622

Note: A list of County Ecumenical Officers names and addresses is available from the Churches Together in England (South) office.

Churches Together in England (Field Officer for North and Midlands)
Crookes Valley Methodist Church
Crookesmoor Road
Sheffield S6 3FQ
Tel : 0114 268 2151

The Council of Churches for Britain and Ireland (CCBI)
Inter-Church House
35-41 Lower Marsh
London SE1 7RL
Tel : 0171 620 4444

CYTUN (Churches Together in Wales)
21 St Helen's Road
Swansea
SA1 4AP
Tel : 01792 460 876

ENFYS
2 Woodland Place
Penarth
CF64 2EX
Tel : 01222 708 234

BIBLIOGRAPHY (England)

Title	Available from
A HARMONY OF CHURCH ADMINISTRATION: Basil W Hazledine Concerning the Inauguration and Operation of Local Ecumenical Projects CCLEPE 1990)	CTE, Inter-Church House 35–41 Lower Marsh London SE1 7RL (£2.95 + 75 p&p)
A HARMONY OF CHURCH FINANCE: Basil W Hazledine With special reference to Local Ecumenical Partnerships	CTE, Inter-Church House 35–41 Lower Marsh London SE1 7RL (£2.95 + 75 p&p)
BAPTISM, EUCHARIST AND MINISTRY (WCC 1982)	CCBI Bookroom Inter-Church House 35-41 Lower Marsh London SE1 7RL (£3.25 + £1.05 p&p)
CONFIRMATION AND RE-AFFIRMATION OF BAPTISMAL FAITH (Joint Liturgical Group 1992)	CCBI Bookroom Inter-Church House 35-41 Lower Marsh London SE1 7RL (£2.50 + 75p p&p)
CONSTITUTIONAL GUIDELINES FOR A LOCAL ECUMENICAL PROJECT An interim document (Group for Local Unity 1993)	CTE, Inter-Church House 35-41 Lower Marsh London SE1 7RL (80p + 40p p&p)

CHURCHES TOGETHER IN MARRIAGE
(CTE 1994)

CTE, Inter-Church House
35-41 Lower Marsh
London SE1 7RL
(£2.50 + 75p p&p)

CHURCHES TOGETHER IN
PILGRIMAGE
(Marigold Book)
(BCC + CTS 1989)

CTE, Inter-Church House
35–41 Lower Marsh
London SE1 7RL
(50p + 75p p&p)

DIRECTORY FOR THE APPLICATION
OF PRINCIPLES AND NORMS ON
ECUMENISM
(revised Roman Catholic Ecumenical
Directory)
(Catholic Truth Society, 1993)

CCBI Bookroom
Inter-Church House
35–41 Lower Marsh
London SE1 7RL
(£3.75 + £1.05 p&p)

ECUMENICAL RELATIONS
Canons B43 and B44: Code of Practice
(General Synod, Church of England 1989)

Church House Bookshop
31 Great Smith Street
London SW1P 3BU
(£2.75 + 75p p&p)

GUIDELINES FOR THE REVIEW OF
LOCAL ECUMENICAL PROJECTS
(revised version)
(CTE 1993)

CTE, Inter-Church House
35-41 Lower Marsh
London SE1 7RL
(£1.00 + 40p p&p)

GUIDELINES ON RECOGNISED AND
REGARDED AND AUTHORISED
STATUS FOR MINISTERS AND
DEACONS OF OTHER CHURCHES
(Methodist Church 1994)

The Methodist Church
Conference Office
25 Marylebone Road
London NW1 5JR
(35p inc p&p)

OPPORTUNITIES FOR UNITY
(Council for Christian Unity)

Church House Bookshop
31 Great Smith Street
London SW1P 3BU
(50p + 50p p&p)

PASTORAL MEASURE
CODE OF RECOMMENDED PRACTICE
(1983)

Church House Bookshop
31 Great Smith Street
London SW1P 3BU
(£4.00 + £1.50 p&p)

PATTERNS OF SHARING AND
COMMITMENT BETWEEN
METHODIST AND
UNITED REFORMED CHURCHES
(6th Edition 1990)

Methodist Publishing House
20 Ivatt Way
Peterborough PE3 7PG
(£.00 + 30p p&p)

(THE) SHARING AND SALE OF
CHURCH BUILDINGS
(CTE 1994)

CTE, Inter-Church House
35-41 Lower Marsh
London SE1 7RL
(30p + 40p p&p)

THIS GROWING UNITY
A handbook on ecumenical development
in the counties, large cities and new towns
of England
Roger Nunn
(CTE 1995)

CCBI Bookroom
Inter-Church House
35–41 Lower Marsh
London SE1 7RL
(£4.95 + £1.25 p&p)

UNDER THE SAME ROOF
Guidelines to the Sharing of Church
Buildings Act 1969
(CCBI in assoc. with CTE & CYTUN 1994)

CCBI Bookroom,
Inter-Church House
35–41 Lower Marsh
London SE1 7RL
(£4.95 + £1.25 p&p)

WAYS OF WORKING TOGETHER
Information and questions for ecumenical
leadership
(Council for Christian Unity)

Church House Bookshop
31 Great Smith Street
London SW1P 3BU
London SW1P 3BU
(£2.50 + 75p p&p)

BIBLIOGRAPHY (Wales)

Available From ENFYS (for address see Appendix 8)

A LIST OF INTER-CHURCH INITIATIVES IN WALES (updated regularly, published jointly with CYTUN) A register of LEPs and other partnerships, listing locations, types and participating Churches.

A SERVICE OF AFFIRMATION AND OF REAFFIRMATION OF FAITH (1994) For use on suitable occasions at united services locally, as well as for services of Joint Confirmation in LEPs, with appendices on Confirmation, Children and Communion, and on a Programme of Precommitment Training.

BAPTISM (1990) An order of service based on the premise that Christian Baptism is one and that both believers' baptism and infant baptism spring from this unity.

CHRISTIAN BAPTISM AND CHURCH MEMBERSHIP (1994, two volumes) The fundamental belief outlined in these volumes is that it is through baptism that we become members of the body of Christ and receive the strength of God's Holy Spirit.

MINISTRY IN A UNITING CHURCH: FROM RECOGNITION TO RECONCILIATION (1986) Patterns of ministry in a Uniting Church in outline, and steps towards the inauguration of a Scheme of Union to bring it about.

THE HOLY COMMUNION (1981) Apart from its use at united services on specific occasions, this Covenanted rite has been given even wider currency as the normative form authorised for the Eucharist in LEPs where the Church in Wales is a participant.

THE HOLY COMMUNION SUPPLEMENT (1993) Provides variety for those who use Covenanted rite of The Holy Communion regularly, as well as for those who may wish to be innovative from time to time.

Available From the Church of Wales
(for address see Appendix 8)

A SUMMARY OF THE LOCAL ECUMENICAL PROJECTS CANON 1991. A pamphlet explaining what is possible Eucharistically and in other ways for Anglican parishes in Wales entering into local partnerships with Churches of other denominations.

CHURCH UNITY? (1992, a Penarth Paper) Church Unity is very dear to some Christians, less important to others. This Paper explores the history of our divisions and of our growth together, to reveal why unity should be of real and urgent concern to Christians at the end of the twentieth century.

PEOPLE WITH CONNECTIONS (1994) A 25 minute video featuring some Local Ecumenical Partnerships in Wales, from Shared Buildings to Joint Confirmations.

THE HEALING OF MEMORIES (1988) An occasional paper showing how our memories are bound up with the question of power and identity, and arguing that the acceptance of the memories of others can be liberating.